# DEATH OF A MUSIC?

# DEATH OF A MUSIC?

*The Decline of the European Tradition*
*and the Rise of Jazz*

by

## HENRY PLEASANTS

LONDON
VICTOR GOLLANCZ LTD
1961

*Printed in Great Britain by*
*The Camelot Press Ltd., London and Southampton*

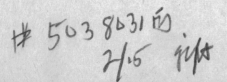

# CONTENTS

# INTRODUCTION

Everyone agrees that something is wrong with contemporary music. There is, however, no agreement about what is wrong, or at least about where to lay the blame. Everyone agrees that something should be done about it, but there is no agreement about what should be done.

It is my own view that things are a lot worse than most people think they are and by no means as bad as they seem. I doubt that anything can be done about it, and I believe also that a great deal has already been done.

I shall try to demonstrate that these opinions are not as self-contradictory as they must appear to be, and that our musical life, while it may present a dismal aspect when seen from one point of view, may appear quite differently when seen from another.

There are in the western world today—and I think that most students of the subject will agree—two dominant musical idioms enjoying the enthusiasm of a large audience of discriminating listeners. These are the idioms known as serious (or classical) music and jazz. The former refers to European music of the preceding centuries and that music of the present century written by Europeans and others in an effort to perpetuate the European tradition. Jazz, as I shall employ the term, refers to the art-music that has emerged only comparatively recently from the turbulent and disordered ferment of a variety of indigenous American popular music. Each of the two idioms is beset by a complex of problems that has been accumulating around it in the course of our century so far.

For serious music the basic problem, and the one from which all others derive, is the fact that the audience served by today's excellent executive serious musical artists prefers old music—old, that is, in the sense that it is not music of today, and hardly even of yesterday.

It is not that there have been no notable new works, compositions that have had some success with the public, have provoked discussion and enjoyed critical acclaim. It is rather that few, if any, of these later works have established themselves as a consistent attraction for a paying public. With the best will in the world, the audience for serious music has been unable to accept the music of contemporary composers as its own music. Even such works as *Le Sacré du Printemps*, *Wozzeck*, and *Pierre Lunaire*, all now nearly half a century old, are still thought of as "modern"—in other words, as strange. That music fifty years old should be thought of as modern is something new in the history of music.

The serious musical community has tended to blame the public, the managers or the composers, according to the position or disposition of the person laying the blame. The managers are charged with greed and selfishness because they favour music that serves or at least does not damage their financial interests. The public is charged with laziness, with closing its ears to the unfamiliar, with failing to make the effort required to meet the composer half-way. And the composers are blamed for writing music unintelligible or disagreeable to the listening public.

I doubt whether any person or group is to blame. There is no reason why the manager or promoter should be required to finance unwanted music from his own pocket. Nor is there any reason why municipal, state or national subsidies should be used to underwrite composers who do not please a sizeable proportion of those who pay the subsidies. Nor should the public be expected to pay at the box-office for music from which it derives no pleasure.

Least of all is the composer to blame. If he writes music that gives some pleasure, or which at least gives no offence, he finds himself rewriting his forerunners and is charged with lack of originality. If he continues in the direction set by Wagner, Strauss and Bruckner, in the direction of further relaxation of the traditional tonal relationships, he is credited with being original and progressive, he becomes a recognized modern, but he writes beyond the capacity or will of his listeners to participate. His music gives no pleasure at all to a considerable number of people, even among the serious-music audience for which he writes.

The serious-music problem, then, is stagnation. Serious music is still the most popular music in the world. The masterpieces of its repertoire enjoy a more enduring and possibly even a wider popularity than any popular music. But there is no renewal. One wonders for how many more generations the masterpieces can stand up to constant repetition.

The world of jazz, on the other hand, is confronted with an entirely different complex of problems. Because of its origin in popular music, and because of the influence that it has exerted upon popular music, it is commonly identified with popular music and regarded, accordingly, as inferior to serious music. It is an indisputably contemporary music, and it has an enormous world-wide audience, but it has no social or artistic status.

It is a self-contained, complete musical society, with its own lay enthusiasts, its own instrumental virtuosos and singers, its own composers, its own concert halls, its own conventions of programme building, its own terminology, its own critics and its own factions.

But its lay enthusiasts are recruited from the young, and their enthusiasm is often obstreperous. Its instrumental virtuosos play strange new instruments such as the saxophones, vibraharp and bongos, and play such older instruments as trumpet, trombone, drums, piano, guitar and double bass in a new and undignified way. Its singers sing popular songs and are dependent upon the microphone. Its composers are thought of as song-writers and arrangers. Its concert halls are night clubs. Its terminology is a chapter of American slang. Its critics use this terminology, write in the vernacular, and refer to the great personalities of jazz by their first names or nicknames. None of this suggests the applicability of the criteria by which we are accustomed to measure a musical idiom's claim to consideration as an art-music.

And yet these criteria are, indeed, all present, and the standards by which they are applied are high. The jazz enthusiast is as critically exacting as his serious-music counterpart, sometimes, probably, even more so. Having less tradition to go on, he is less inhibited by traditional precepts and conventions, and less inclined to accept reputation on faith. The accomplishments of the jazz instrumentalists are admittedly extraordinary. The skill of the arrangers is acknowledged. Singers of serious music, if not their public, recognize the superior quality of the phrasing and vocalism in the work of an Ella Fitzgerald or of a Frank Sinatra. The best of the song-writers, whose products comprise the basic repertoire of the jazz musician or singer, enjoy worldwide renown and respect—as song-writers!

The jazz problem is, thus, not one of contemporaneity or renewal. It is rather one of recognition and acceptance as a new art-music. It must dissociate itself in the public mind and in the mind of the serious-music world from the trivia of the Hit Parade and the workaday dance-band. It must dissociate itself also from the primitiveness of early jazz, however great its debt to the founding fathers. And it must dissociate itself from dope addiction and juvenile delinquency. The problem is of incalculable difficulty and complexity, since the derogatory associations and prejudices are deeply imbedded in what the world in general—and the serious-music world in particular—thinks of jazz, and since within the jazz community itself there is no agreement as to where the lines are to be drawn which separate jazz from popular music or one kind of jazz from another. Outside the jazz community few know enough even to know that such problems and confusions exist.

It would appear that we are faced, musically, in this century, not with one evolutionary crisis, but two; or at least with an evolutionary crisis consisting of two main divisions. With serious music the problem is to identify and understand the nature of its stagnation, the causes and the consequences. With jazz the problem is to identify, first, those elements of style which set it off so distinctly from the main body of western music, and then those elements of both quality and style which set it off from the main body of American popular music. In the following chapters I propose to examine these problems separately, and ultimately to arrive at some general conclusions relating each part of the crisis to the other and applicable to the evolutionary crisis as a whole.

# PART I

# THE CRISES OF EVOLUTION IN EUROPEAN MUSIC

"The sign of all living art, the pure harmony of 'will', 'must' and 'can', the self-evidence of the aim, the un-self-consciousness of the execution, the unity of the art and the Culture—all that is past and gone. . . . What is practised as art today—be it music after Wagner or painting after Cezanne, Leibl and Menzel—is impotence and falsehood."

OSWALD SPENGLER[1]

# THE COMPOSER AND HIS AUDIENCE

THE LATE Artur Honegger in his monograph, *Je suis Compositeur*,[2] described the contemporary composer's situation as bluntly as possible, and about as honestly.

"The profession of composer," he wrote, "discloses the singularity . . . of a person who troubles himself to produce something for which there are no consumers. . . . The contemporary composer is a gate-crasher trying to push his way into a company to which he has not been invited."

Honegger offers us, in other words, the familiar spectacle of the contemporary composition sandwiched between Beethoven and Brahms, of the gate-crasher sneaking into the concert hall under the coat tails of the elect. We can even imagine the conductor's part in the conspiracy. There is Beethoven on one side to make sure that the audience comes in, and there is Brahms on the other to make sure that it does not get out until the gate-crasher has been heard.

It is an accurate picture, but unfair to the poor composer. Not many people like his music very much, but at the same time his gate-crashing is not deeply resented. The audience for serious music prefers the older European music with which it is familiar, but at the same time it is loath to assume that nothing of any consequence may yet be added to the repertoire. The persistent presence of the gate-crasher, even after fifty years of failure, is evidence that while there is life, or even a gate-crasher, there is hope.

The serious musical community's hopeful tolerance is

encouraged by the assiduous propagation and wide acceptance of the legend of the composer unappreciated in his own
time. For the layman who finds tolerance difficult there is
offered the spectre of a future generation's rapture and the
implied suggestion that to voice derogatory opinions is to
risk going down in history as an ass. The layman overlooks
a droll contradiction. While being reminded of earlier
generations' alleged failures to appreciate their own composers, he is also rebuked for not displaying their eager
appetite for new music.

Thanks to this kind of propaganda, the contemporary
composer enjoys an activity in his own behalf, a predis-
position in his favour, never enjoyed by the composers from
whose music the standard repertoire is still drawn. Prizes,
awards, fellowships, grants, commissions, festivals, subsidies and indulgent criticism assist him on his way. Promoters occasionally accept deficits, performers tax the
patience of their listeners, and listeners listen dutifully,
all in order that our musical society may not in the future
be charged with failure to support the composers of its
own time.

I am certain to be reminded here of the assistance and
promotion received by various famous composers of the
eighteenth and nineteenth centuries from royal patronage
and wealthy sponsorship. Well, some received it and some
did not. Nor should it be assumed that such sponsorship was
always enlightened. More often it was conservative, casual,
indifferent and frustrating. But what all the composers had
in common, whose names and works have come down to us,
was success, sooner or later, with a large paying public.
The size of the public may have varied, but it was numerous
enough to identify the composer's music as representative

of his own culture. In every case the composer succeeded with the public at which he was aiming, regardless of the question of his financial rewards, sometimes enormous, sometimes meagre. Often enough he succeeded in the face of critical opposition, competitive intrigue and bureaucratic obstruction. But audiences, not critics or bureaucrats, determine the tastes of a culture or period.

As put by a correspondent of *The Times* of August 22, 1959, "Contrary to the romantic novelette or film conception of the matter, very few—if any—of the great creative geniuses of the past have ever been left totally unrecognized by their blind and uncomprehending fellow men. Several have not received their full financial deserts (and here Mozart immediately comes to mind) and several of more inquiring mind have at first foxed even their staunchest admirers with some innovatory extension of the existing vocabulary.

"Beethoven's 'Rasumovsky' quartets were described by a reputable contemporary critic as 'very long and difficult . . . deep in thought and well worked out but not generally comprehensible'. Schubert's enchanting miniatures were similarly dismissed as mere aphoristic and fragmentary 'revellings in strangeness', and even Schumann himself, incensed by the consecutive fifths and octaves in 'Tannhäuser', deplored the fact that Wagner 'cannot write or imagine four consecutive bars that are melodious or even correct'. Countless more examples could be quoted to prove Jean Cocteau's contention that 'when a work of art seems in advance of its generation, the truth of the matter is that its generation is behind it'.

"Yet there were always the Rossinis and Donizettis who could scarcely keep pace with the public demand for new works from their pens, and even in the case of those composers of more inquiring mind, their fellow men seem always to have caught up just in time to applaud some measure of their genius without first securely nailing them in their coffins. Always, that is, until the present day. . . ."

Despite such testimony to its fraudulence—and the history of western music is one long chain of additional evidence—the legend of the composer unappreciated in his own time persists. Society prefers the "romantic novelette or film conception of the matter", and the contemporary composer benefits from it. But, in the end, he is no better off. The stupendous accomplishments of his predecessors, and the popularized dramatizations of their adversities, may have earned him a semi-privileged place in society. They may have given to his profession the aura of a special calling and a special immunity, placing him outside the vulgar workings of the law of supply and demand. But they have also imposed upon him lofty objectives which, since Beethoven's time, succeeding generations of composers have found it ever harder to achieve. It is no longer sufficient for a composer simply to please; somehow he must also enlighten and elevate, or at least mystify. Above all things he must be original and he must avoid triviality. He must communicate with an audience and with critics who find easy communication suspect.

His problem is rooted in the now widely accepted concept of music as something to be "understood", and in the corollary assumption that music difficult to understand is more profound and therefore superior to that which is more easily understood. Probably no other word is used so often in the discussion of music as "understanding". Certainly no other is used with less precision.

The notion that music is something to be understood persists although no one has ever defined precisely what it is that one is supposed to understand. It is possible, of course, to understand the form of a composition, the elements of melody, harmony and rhythm that go into it, and the techniques by which its structure is achieved. But this is not what is usually meant by understanding.

The implication is rather of indefinable meaning than of definable structure. Music is assumed to convey to the initiated an intelligible communication, preferably of philosophical character. The language of criticism and commentary abounds in such terms as thought, depth, struggle, conflict, suffering, solitude, confession, obscurity, enigma, reflection, introspection, imagination, lucidity, fantasy, mystery, idea, sentiment, communion, description, expression, spirituality, dream, picture, poem, etc.

The terminology derives from the subjective character of the great representative music of the nineteenth century, which was dominated, musically, by Germans and by German philosophical thoughts and habits. This is music of the era loosely described as romantic. It comprises by far the greater part of the standard repertoire. It is the music for which the great majority of serious-music lovers have an uninhibited preference, and it is the music to which they refer when they speak of serious, or, even more loosely, classical music.

In so far as the layman understands it, or thinks that he understands it, he does so in terms of the philosophical, psychological, mystical, and biographical interpretation that is the substance of such professional criticism, appreciation, and commentary as come his way. The interpretation of the opening measures of Beethoven's Fifth Symphony as representing fate knocking at the door is a serviceable example.

Such discussion is not and cannot be precise. No two critics or commentators agree on the substantive meaning of any given piece. Often enough, two analyses, even by two composers, may yield diametrically opposed conclusions. Thus the layman is confronted with a mystery.

He may be aware that the mystery is insoluble even to the professionals. But he modestly assumes that they are closer to enlightenment than he, and thus honours them with the respect due to the initiated. Among the latter the composer, being closest to the mystery, the chosen instrument for the propagation of its enigmas, emerges as a sort of high priest, a man ordained to communicate with the Infinite, a source of spiritual and cultural enrichment and, as such, deserving of the encouragement and support of the less sublimely endowed. He is also assumed to know better than society what is good for it, musically, and is, thus, not only permitted, but even encouraged to write his own ticket.

The result is to separate the composer from society, or at least to free him of concern for the tastes of even that segment of society which constitutes the audience for serious music. In free societies he is assumed to be responsible only to his art as it is interpreted by what he calls his artistic integrity. In totalitarian societies he is simply held responsible to his government for the manner in which he responds to his calling. In neither case does a popular estimate of his value, on the evidence of enthusiasm for his product—even from the serious-music audience to which it is addressed—carry any weight.

Curiously, the masterpieces of the standard repertoire date from periods when the relationship of artist to audience was quite the reverse. In the seventeenth, eighteenth and even the nineteenth centuries gifted composers were numerous. Their purpose was to please, and to prosper from approval. The musical art took its place among other crafts and professions, and society was not disposed to confuse musical invention with revelation.

Bach, Handel, Mozart, and even Beethoven all worked at composition for a living. They were expected to give their employers and benefactors what the latter wanted. They did, *also musi-cians* and not always without compromise. They wrote the kind of music that was fashionable in the society whose tastes and habits shaped the cultural profile of the time. They worked in a common style, or musical language, understood by musician and listener alike. They wrote because there was a demand for their product, and distinguished themselves by writing better than their contemporaries.

The same was true of many later composers who wrote for a less restricted audience and usually without any benevolent sponsorship at all. Rossini, Donizetti, Bellini, Meyerbeer, Weber, Verdi and Puccini all made a handsome living from composing operas. Even Wagner seldom suffered from lack of popularity. His difficulties were in getting his works produced, not in getting them liked. *NY?*

Among the non-opera composers, Schubert, Mendelssohn, Schumann, Chopin, Liszt and Brahms all derived a sizeable proportion of their incomes from commissioned compositions and the sale of their published works. What they earned additionally as teachers, virtuosos and conductors was directly related to the fame and popularity derived from their compositions. The same held true right down to our own time in the circumstances of such initially popular composers as Strauss, Ravel and Stravinsky.

In other words, our view of the composer as independent of the law of supply and demand, as a sort of autonomous ornament of society, is of recent origin. Previously the composer was regarded as a working professional. His prosperity and renown were determined, as in other walks of life, by what society, uninhibited in its judgment, thought of his work. Now, as the successor of a long line of composers whose accomplishments were extraordinary, he is accorded an extraordinary position.

Since composers, superstition to the contrary notwithstanding, are only human, it is hardly surprising that in the light of this reverence for their calling they should be inclined to accept their privileged position as no less than their due and be tempted to the kind of arrogance reflected by Roger Sessions in *The Musical Experience*.[3]

"What does the listener demand from music?" he asks. "The answer will inevitably be that a variety of listeners want a variety of things. But on any level it may be taken for granted that the listener wants vital experience, whether of a deeply stirring, brilliantly stimulating or simply entertaining type. If we understand this we should understand, too, that the composer can effectively furnish it only on his own terms. He can persuade others to love only what he loves himself, and convince only by means of what fully convinces him. It is for this reason that the artist must be completely free, that such a question as I have just stated here can ultimately have no importance to him."

Elsewhere in this book Mr. Sessions states: "Without this complete freedom for the artist to create according to his impulses, there can be no development. Music, or any art, can in such a case only follow the law of the lowest common denominator; in providing the public with 'what it wants' it will inexorably tend to provide it with what is understood with least effort."

Aaron Copland has carried this attitude a step farther. What the audience wants is to him not only of no importance: it is also of no interest. Thus, in his *Music and Imagination*,[4] he can write without embarrassment: "Parenthetically I should like to call attention to a curious bit of artist psychology. The thought that my music might or might not give pleasure to a considerable number of music lovers has never particularly stirred me."

Here Copland is possibly echoing Schönberg, who said, in his *Style and Idea*,[5] "I believe that a real composer writes for no other purpose than to please himself. Those who compose because they want to please others and have audiences in mind are not real artists."

One is reminded of Haydn, who once wrote to a group of admirers: "You give me the pleasant conviction . . . that I am often the enviable source from which you and so many families susceptible of true feeling derive pleasure and enjoyment in domestic life. What happiness does this thought cause me!"[6]

Or we have Mozart, writing to his father from Paris, July 3, 1778, about the performance of his Symphony (K. 297): "I prayed God that it might go well, for it is all to His greater honour and glory and behold—the symphony began. . . . Just in the middle of the first Allegro there was a passage which I felt sure must please. The audience was quite carried away—and there was a tremendous burst of applause. But as I knew when I wrote it what effect it would surely produce, I had introduced the passage again at the close—when there were shouts of 'Da capo!' The Andante also found favour . . . but particularly the last Allegro. . . . The audience, as I expected, said 'hush' at the soft beginning, and, when they heard the forte, began at once to clap their hands. I was so happy that as soon as the symphony was over, I went off to the Palais Royal, where I had a large ice, said the rosary as I had vowed to do —and went home. . . ."[7]

Neither Haydn's nor Mozart's is the language of men for whom what the listener demands from music was "of no importance", nor of men who were not stirred by the thought that their music might give pleasure to a considerable number of listeners, nor of men for whom composers who want to please others and have audiences in mind were not real artists. Or did Schönberg, perhaps, think that Haydn and Mozart were not real artists?

If we compare their attitude with that of Sessions, Copland and Schönberg, we gain some idea of where two centuries of composer-idolatry have taken us in the eyes of the composers. We have earned it! The serious musical community accepts this disgusting amalgam of conceit, self-importance, contempt and defiance placidly and even applauds it.

It is not surprising, however, in view of such attitudes on the part of composers, that applause smacks more of contrite obeisance than of spontaneous affection. The composer notes the deficiency and, despite his protestations of indifference to anyone's opinion or pleasure except his own, turns to his fellows for more congenial approval. As Hindemith has put it in his *A Composer's World*: "You meet with your fellow sufferers in international, national and local societies for contemporary music; you arrange festivals, symposia, and anything else for the propaganda of your products and those of your fellow highbrows."[10]

If such insights, even coming, as they do, from composers themselves, seem to present the composer in a ludicrously pompous posture, it should be reiterated that his public does not find it unseemly, and that his troubles arise not only from his own pretentiousness, but also from the pretensions thrust upon him by the flower of his family tree and the folklore of musical appreciation. He can no longer be a popular composer, even if he would.

He is identified with a tradition that commends, not popularity, but significance; not conformity with a style, reflecting the collective voice of society, but a style of his own, reflecting the intimate voice of his own inspiration. He dare not be popular, or even readily accessible, for popular and accessible music is assumed to be synonymous with light or easy music, and therefore inferior. The composer is, by definition, serious. His tradition requires—by contemporary interpretation, at any rate—not success with his public, but a reputation for greatness, or at least originality, with his fellows—and the critics.

This is the answer to those who are tempted to argue that the solution to the problem of modern music is for the contemporary composer to come down out of his ivory tower and write a couple of good tunes. It is not so simple. Whether the composer comes down of his own accord, as happens from time to time in free societies, or is hauled down as happens in totalitarian societies, the result, even when successful, is not entirely satisfying. The free western composer cannot leave his tower without hazarding his status as a serious composer. A totalitarian government cannot compel the composer to leave it without subjecting him to the same jeopardy—and itself, too. By forcing him to compromise himself as a serious composer, it requires that he dissipate those very qualities that earn him respect both at home and abroad and thus constitute a large part of his propaganda value.

Not even a system as autocratic as that of the Soviet Union can control the evolution of social forces, or, for that matter, escape them; and the evolution of music is inseparable from social evolution. Those who have modestly undertaken to direct the cultural destiny of the Soviet masses proceed from the identical error that so confuses musical thought in the western world. This is the assumption that public taste can be determined or directed by outside agencies—either composers or critics or governments.

Granted that in highly developed musical societies certain composers have stood out above their fellows and have seemed to make musical history. But this has occurred at the height rather than at the beginning of major epochs, and has been valid only as long as the product and its stylistic consequences have met the approval of the society for which it was produced. The symbol of prosperity is a flourishing style, not a brilliant individual or a group of individuals. It is society's verdict as expressed in the popular acceptance of a style, not the composer's individuality as expressed in a masterpiece, that determines the course of musical history. Style provides the foundation without which masterpieces are impossible, or at least unlikely.

The contemporary composer likes to talk about writing the music of his own time, about reflecting through his superior musical endowment and intellect the society into which he had been born. But, since he ignores and even scorns his audience, he forgoes the foundation of a socially confirmed style, and is condemned to build castles in the air—or in the sand. His music is modern only in the sense that it is written in the present. It is identifiable as modern only in the sense that it resembles, more or less, the music of other men of similar aspirations and similar prejudices. It expresses nothing but his own incapacity to grasp, or his unwillingness to face up to, the musician's communicative responsibility. Communication requires an identification with the target of communication—the audience—a respect for its wishes, a compulsion to cater to its pleasures and the humility to rejoice in its approval. This is clearly not for the contemporary composer,

His is not the music of modern society, and it never will be: though the serious-music audience would like to think that it has its own new music, and is disposed to take an indulgent view of what is offered as such. Nor would the serious-music audience be likely to approve if it were, for what is popular is now suspect unless hallowed by age. The composer may draw upon popular sources, as the saying goes, but he must submit them to intellectual processing. The thumbscrews of modern harmony and the rack of modern orchestration are considered to be an essential purifying ritual in the preparation of popular musical elements for a condition of cultural grace.

In free societies the audience may complain about the music, and the composer about the audience; in totalitarian societies the state may order the composer to write more popularly, and the composer may mutter under his breath about the iniquities of party bureaucracy. Nothing can be done about it in either case. The composer is both bene-ficiary and victim of an audience which wants to like him but expects him to be difficult. Competing with the masterpieces, he is expected to produce masterpieces, and lacking the flourishing style, the socially confirmed contemporary idiom that produced the masterpieces, he cannot oblige.

He no longer works within the rhetorical conventions of the great nineteenth-century German style, for it is no longer a contemporary idiom, but he has inherited its structural and expressive frame of reference—and is stuck with it. He has inherited the structural tools and the expressive purposes, and they are rather the worse for wear. It is here, I believe, in the composer's struggle with his inherited materials and his inherited purposes, that we may come closer to the secret of the stagnation of serious music than is possible by any effort to explain it all away by blaming the composer for his arrogance, the audience for its indifference or hopeful discontent, or the manager and impresario for their failure to sponsor the new music.

# THE COMPOSER AND HIS MATERIALS

## I

## HARMONY

THIS MATERIAL INHERITANCE would appear, at first glance, to be enviable.

Three centuries of exploration and development have left the composer with a harmonic language fully developed and finally free even of such conventions as still governed the composition of the late nineteenth-century German masters. In the symphony orchestra he has the grandest and most exquisitely organized collective musical instrument the world has ever known. He has a variety of forms, from sonata to symphony, from song to opera, from motet to oratorio, all of demonstrated viability. If his singers are, perhaps, inferior to those of older times, the instrumentalists at his disposal are superior in technical skill and in the general standard of their musicianship to those for whom his predecessors wrote, and their instruments, excepting only the strings, are superior to the instruments of any past era. And yet precisely the wealth of his inherited materials confronts the contemporary composer with his ultimate and most perplexing embarrassment, what Honegger has called "a wall of accumulated materials".[2]

Most composers agree that multiple-voiced tonal harmony, organized in a system of related keys, or tonalities, is what sets off western music so distinctively from all other musical systems; constituting the fountainhead of its lyrical and dramatic resources and providing a frame of reference

of expressive purpose and structural means hitherto accepted
and understood by composer and listener alike. It has been
within this frame of reference that all the European masterpieces have been accomplished. And it is within this frame
of reference that the contemporary composer first looked for
the fresh materials required for fresh masterpieces. In this
he was simply following the example of his predecessors.

The history of European music tells us how composers
and their listeners, starting tentatively from the diatonic
harmony that superseded modal polyphony at the beginning
of the seventeenth century, discovered the structural and
dramatic implications of this new harmony; they codified
its resources, established the conventions governing their
exploitation, and then pushed on, in the nineteenth century,
to explore the graphic, reflective and subtler dramatic
properties of diatonic harmony's chromatic extensions.

A Bach, a Handel, a Haydn and a Mozart, after a century
and a half of experiment and codification, could work within
a generally accepted harmonic syntax, challenging convention enough to stimulate excitement, but excelling
primarily by the brilliance of their invention within the
disciplines established by their forerunners and the limitations set by their listeners' expectations. After them came
the headier excitement of the age of chromatic exploration,
when individual composers, defying the conventional
bounds of harmonic manœuvre, each staked out his own
claim and established his own style in the exploitation of the
new properties.

Audiences found all this fascinating. Contrary to the
folklore of musical appreciation, it was an eagerness on the
part of the audience for novelty and excitement that drove
the nineteenth-century pioneers on to ever more daring

efforts. It was no longer sufficient for a composer to work well within a common style or discipline. He had to be individual and original. The result was an infectious disregard of the older conventions and an accelerated exploitation of every new harmonic find. The experience of the past fifty years indicates that there are now no new unexplored areas within the bounds of tonal harmony, diatonic or chromatic.

What this has meant to the composer in the twentieth century is nowhere better illustrated than in the careers of those who, in the first decade, completed the job of exploration by their probings in the outermost limits of tonal space. It is possible to attribute the apparent barrenness of some of the younger men to lack of talent. At least, their talent has not been demonstrated by enduring success with the audience for serious music. But what is one to say of those who, in the early years of the century, established their ability to compose music of popular appeal? One thinks particularly of such men at Strauss, Schönberg, Stravinsky, Ravel and Puccini.

In nothing he wrote afterwards was Strauss able to achieve the popular success of the tone poems and the early operas, *Salome* and *Der Rosenkavalier*. Schönberg never again wrote music as appealing as the *Gurrelieder* and *Verklaerte Nacht*. Stravinsky's most popular works remain *The Firebird* and *Petrouchka*. Ravel's masterpiece is the comparatively early *Daphnis and Chloe*. Puccini could never surpass the success of *La Bohème*, *Madame Butterfly* and *Tosca*.

All this music preceded the First World War, and was written when the composers were comparatively young men. It can hardly have been that they suddenly lost their talent.

It seems more likely, even certain, that their inherited structural resources simply ran out on them, or at least that they could no longer be expanded within the inherited tonal frame of reference. The composer's apparently rich inheritance had proved to be a worked-out mine, with all tributary veins pursued to the end. He had been left, in short, with a slag-heap.

In order to understand the extent of the débâcle and the full implications of the composer's predicament, it is necessary to examine more closely the harmonic basis of European music and the influence of harmonic considerations on such other structural elements as melody, rhythm and instrumentation. I have referred previously to the concept of music as something to be understood, suggesting that herein lies the key to what we mean when we speak of serious music. The implication is that serious music means something and that it must mean something, or seem to, in order to qualify as music worth taking seriously—as something superior to music that merely entertains.

I believe that this meaning, or appearance of meaning, derives from the structural tensions produced by great composers, and particularly by the great German composers, through the dramatic exploitation of the tensions implicit in the relationship of individual notes to other notes within those keys that constitute the tonal frame of reference of western music.

We have always had in western music a dramatic nucleus in our modes and scales. This nucleus exists in the pull of one note towards another, depending upon the position of the tones and semitones in the mode or scale. In our diatonic scale, as it emerged in the seventeenth century, with its sharpened seventh, we have the most dramatic of scales.

The fact that this sharpened seventh is called a "leading-note" speaks for itself. Its pull to the tonic or basic note is the strongest of any we know in the relationship of single notes to other single notes. Its movement to the tonic brings a sense of rest and resolution. Its failure to do so brings a sense of deception, suspense and agitation. In the hazardous sharpening of the seventh, and in the possibilities thereby provided for the creation of suspense or resolution, depending upon the composer's communicative purpose, we have the dramatic nucleus that has nourished the entire production of serious music for three hundred years.

It has, to be sure, been greatly expanded and refined. There are other dramatic relationships among the notes of the diatonic and its associated minor scales. And there are the dramatic key relationships derived from the fact that a new diatonic scale can be built upon any note of the scale. The tensions in these relationships of notes to one another can be augmented by combining the notes in chords, and they can be further exploited in an infinite variety of ways by movements from one chord to another and from one key to another.

In the earlier and more innocent days of our western music, when the listener's sense of tonality was more acute and more sensitive to disturbance than it is today, the journey from one key to another distant key was made through a bridge of related keys. This was done out of consideration for the listener, who would have been deprived of his tonal equilibrium by too long or too sudden a jump from one key to another. But just this element of the hazardous gave the composer his dramatic materials. By modulation from one key to another he was given the variety of tonal material that made extensive structure, and dramatic

B

juxtaposition and contrast, possible. Just as the simple melodist achieves structure by exploiting the dramatic faculties of those steps in the scale known as dominant, sub-dominant, supertonic and leading-note, so the sophisticated European composer could exploit the same dramatic elements, not just in movement from note to note or chord to chord, but in movement from key to key. And by keeping just a bit ahead of his listener's anticipation he could increase his excitement, his sense of suspense and dramatic occurrence.

The listener participated in the composer's bold enterprise, his rash invention, and applauded his accomplishment when all concerned were happily back in the key from which they had departed. There were conflicts along the way between composers and audiences and between composers and critics as to what constituted the limit to which the composer might go in deceiving his listener's anticipations. Composers accused their listeners of laziness, as they do today, and listeners accused the composers of recklessness, capriciousness and unintelligibility, but despite such outbreaks of impatience and exasperation, the system worked. The composer, by constantly giving the listener something beyond that to which he was accustomed, held his interest, and the listener, by his protests at too radical a procedure, kept the composer mindful of his obligations to his audience.

In the latter half of the nineteenth century composers became increasingly heedless in their exploitation of harmonic suspense and tension. Progressions and modulations became more and more adventurous and more and more arbitrary. This was partly because of the growing emphasis on descriptive music. It was found that certain radical progressions and changes of key produced impressionistic effects of contrast, colour and shade. It was also partly because audiences demanded more and more excitement. In Berlioz, Liszt, Brahms, Wagner, Strauss and Bruckner they were served plenty. But they paid a price in jaded ears and numbed sensibilities. Wagner and Strauss may still seem exciting today, but the excitement can be nothing compared with that experienced by those who heard this music when it was new. How long it will remain exciting at all is something for the organizers of our concerts to ponder.

But to return to our contemporary composer, he inherited a tonal frame of reverence where he was free to do as he pleased. He was no longer inhibited by rules or conventions. Every chord, every progression, every modulation, every abrupt change of key was permissible. But he also inherited an audience similarly uninhibited. This audience could be bored, but it could no longer be shocked. Composer and audience had long since sacrificed the sense of beauty to the sense of excitement, and now even excitement was hard to come by. The composer discovered to his sorrow that where everything goes, nothing matters. His forerunners had successfully outraged the harmonic sensibilities of succeeding generations of listeners to the point where nothing further could be felt as outrageous. A three-hundred-year epoch of musical evolution, characterized by harmonic exploration and discovery, had come to an end.

The implications of this harmonic crisis are not generally grasped by the serious-music audience, and hardly even by the majority of the serious-music critics; but the composers understand them only too well, and have done so for a long time. First, they know what the tensions implicit in tonal harmony have meant to the European composers of the past. Even Schönberg said: "Music depends not only on acoustics but upon logic and upon those particular laws which result from combination of tone and tune. Tonality, tending to render harmonic facts perceptible and correlate them, is therefore not an end but a means."[8] And Krenek has finished the thought by adding: "If tonality is a means, then what is its end? Obviously a general organization of musical material in such a way that musical structures may be comprehended as logically coherent wholes."[9] Hindemith has put it more simply: "The core of all the problems puzzling the composer . . . is the theoretical considerations concerning the nature and technical potentialities of the chordal and tonal progressions which are his material of construction.

"There was in musical history," he continues, "a time when these effects of perspective—or of tonality, as the technical term goes—were unknown to musicians. This was at a time before harmonies were used consciously and when music consisted only of melodic lines. Even nowadays in many countries and cultures that are not under the domination of western musical techniques and habits, harmony is either unknown or flatly rejected as an unwelcome addition to the native material of music, and people with this exclusively melodic conception of music cannot have any effect of the sounding perspective of tonality as expressed by harmonic reference to tonal fundamentals. With harmony it seems to go as with the tree of the knowledge of good and evil; once you have tasted its fruits, you have lost your innocent approach to the facts of life. For us, after our musical development has gone through about a thousand years of musical knowledge that consisted exclusively of harmonized musical structure, it is quite impossible to understand melodic lines without harmonic and tonal implications."[10]

Roger Sessions has come to similar conclusions. "Actually," he has written, "the roots of the technical crisis in music may be traced far back into the past. They may be traced, if one likes, at least to the time when Bach, following the implications of tonality to logical conclusions, advocated the general adoption of the tempered scale. This led, as we all know, to the exploitation of an ever wider circle of key-relationships, and thus made possible the sonata form—what we call sometimes the 'symphonic' technique of Beethoven. The essence of this technique is the possibility it yields of organizing the sharpest contrasts.

"It made possible not only design of the largest possible span, by reason of the far-flung tonal relationships which it put at the composer's disposal, but it yielded also, quite inevitably, a far greater richness of detail on a smaller scale. For as bold juxtapositions of distantly related harmonies became familiar—and as the ear became accustomed to them—it became inevitable that composers should use them with less and less constraint. We may regard the development of music in the nineteenth century as, from one point of view, the result of the fact that composers found such highly charged juxtapositions exciting, and gained from them an apparently inexhaustible supply of new and even subtler nuances of expression. . . .

"As of 1914—the year when the nineteenth century began to collapse—the musical world (the creative musical world, that is) was dominated by Debussy and Richard Strauss, whose music at that time seemed to carry the development of harmony as far as it could be carried within the limits of the tonal system. Strauss had recently written his 'Elektra', and it was not yet evident that in his later works he would turn his back decisively on the harmonic daring and the expressive power which that work embodies. As for Debussy, he at that time considered his work as in some sense an act of rebellion against the confining principles of tonality, widely regarded by composers of that day as an encumbrance which had outlived its usefulness and of which composers had best rid themselves as quickly as possible. . . .

"Music had developed to a point where its formerly valid premises, of which tonality was only one, had collapsed; in a sense they had collapsed of their own weight. The nineteenth century had run its course, and the composers were moved to discover new values to supersede it. . . . It was evident that the flood of new possibilities, or let us say new material, which music had acquired needed organization; that the nineteenth-century development had led to a kind of anarchy for which the prevailing ideas of the time offered no principle of organization. The composers of the twenties felt very clearly that the freedom of resources they had acquired had been yielded ultimately by the classic tradition; that it had developed out of that tradition, which through its own inherent drive, had led beyond itself. It was not a question of repudiating this tradition but of organizing the sequel to it."[3]

This would seem to be a euphemistic way of indicating that the fight for harmonic emancipation turned out to have been a long, lusty crusade for the privilege of committing harmonic suicide. But it was not until they had practically destroyed the implications of tonality that composers suddenly discovered that emancipation had brought them, not

freedom of musical speech, but the inability to speak musically at all. The tonal framework they had so hopefully
destroyed proved to have been the very substance of their
creative language. It was as if man had escaped the constraints of the earth's atmosphere only to discover that he
could no longer breathe and must quickly find or devise
another—or, to return to our composer, "organize a sequel".

There did not seem to be much hope in harmony. As
Hindemith has put it, "If anything seems to be of little
reward, it is the search for originality in harmony. After a
thousand years of research, experiment, and application,
harmony has become thoroughly known; no undiscovered
chord can be found. If we have to depend on novelty in
harmony, we might as well write our last funeral march for
the death of our own music."[10]

And Honegger, reminded of a statement by the French
critic, Emile Vuillermoz, that creative originality lies in the
capacity to produce new harmony, remarked: "Think of
the dead end to which such a formula drives us. If Vuillermoz is right, then that means that there can be no more
great composers, since all possible harmonic superimposi-
tions have already been employed."[2]

The composers, neither individually nor as a body, were
disposed to write "the last funeral march for the death of
their own music". As Sessions has put it: "If we should
allow ourselves to regard music as essentially dead, we
would be confessing not only our inability to cope with its
demands, but our unwillingness to do so. We would be, as
it were, denying our creative impulse or confessing ourselves devoid of it."[3]

The means by which composers have sought to avoid a
denial of their creative impulse are various, but they all have

in common what Honegger noted as "dependence on working methods";[2] presumably another way of saying that they
preceded without reference to their audience and looked to
their own understanding of the technique of composition,
rather than to their listeners, for guidance. The twelve-
tonists felt that the answer to the crisis of harmony was a
systematized atonality. Schönberg, Berg, von Webern and
many others whose names are less familiar to laymen, took
this conclusion as a point of departure. They assumed, not
without some logic, that a musical art whose progress had
been for a century and a half in the direction of a relaxation
of tonal relationships must certainly have an atonal destination. Or, to put it differently, they thought that they could
continue the harmonic tradition by freeing harmony of
tonal reference.

They adhered to the western tradition of part-writing,
but without reference to, and, in defiance of, the feeling for
key and key relationships which had provided the structural
basis of all previous western music. Their syntax derived
from a system of motifs, or twelve-tone rows, rather than a
system of chords and modulations.

Others, headed originally by Stravinsky, thought that
a fusion of modern techniques with classical forms and
expressive concepts might afford an opportunity for further
progress. The neo-classical composers had no difficulty in
persuading themselves that this was neither reactionary in
conception nor retrogressive in practice. As Stravinsky put
it in his *Poetics of Music*: "The true tradition is not the
symbol of a forgotten past; it is a living force that inspires
and instructs the present. . . . One associates oneself with a
tradition in order to create something new."[11]

Indeed, the neo-classicists could even persuade themselves

that they were the real revolutionaries and, by implication, progressive. The return to classical models, as they saw it, represented a revolt against the formal licence and emotional excesses of the late nineteenth century, while their employment of dissonance in the modern manner and of scoring that employed all the assets of the modern orchestra was a guarantee against the charge of antiquarianism or reaction that might otherwise have resulted from such a demonstrated preference for a better ordered past.

In neither case, atonal nor neo-classic, has the result contributed to a lessening of the gap between composer and public. The lay listener has been as little charmed by one as by the other. While the composer has worked out his aesthetic and technical problems on the basis of analyses and deductions, the problem of the composer-listener relationship has gone by default.

Of the two approaches, that of the twelve-tonists is the more radical, despite the superficially plausible argument that the tone-row system is no more than a logical next step in the relaxation of tonal relationships. Only Krenek, however, among its practitioners has pointed to the reason why it is so radical, and he has done so, quite possibly unwittingly. Discussing the neo-classicists, he has written:

"For about twenty years music has been undergoing a reaction against the complexity of atonality and the twelve-tone technique. This reaction is distinguished from similar processes in the past primarily by the fact that it was not introduced by a new generation of composers but rather by the leading composers of an established generation, almost all of whom began complexly and moved towards simplicity. Bartok, Milhaud, Hindemith and Stravinsky may be cited as examples.

"The new simplicity as revealed by both older and younger composers is distinct from similar movements in the past in that it is not restricted to the simplification of structure but reaches back to a previous musical language, namely, tonality. The post-Bach primitives cannot be cited as parallels, since the musical language was not changed. It was tonal both before and after. A hypothetical parallel would have the composers of the seventeenth century, confused by Monteverdi's innovations, going back to the modal style of Palestrina. It is just this effort to recall past circumstances that gives the new simplicity its fatal reactionary flavour."[12]

This is an instructive statement, distinguished not only by critical insight, but also by an uncommonly acute historical perspective. Krenek is certainly correct in his observation of a reaction in favour of simplicity on the part of many composers who began complexly. He is also correct, as far as the neo-classicists are concerned, in noting that this reaction looks to tonality for its salvation. Most astute of all is his recognition of the present crisis as something more profound and far-reaching than any of the various shifts in the trends of composition and popular taste represented by such non-conformists as Gluck, Mozart, Beethoven, Berlioz, Wagner, and Debussy. In these previous crises, as Krenek notes, "The language was not changed. It was tonal both before and after."[12] That what is now involved in atonality or the twelve-tone system is, indeed, a change of language, is the single most important factor to be remembered in any attempt to appraise the situation and condition of contemporary serious music.

It is all very well to say that atonality has been prepared by a long period of tonal disintegration. But this does not mean that the change from a tonal to an atonal musical language is not radical. As long as there is a shred of tonal resource left unexploited by composers, the frame of musical reference is still tonal. But once an atonal frame of reference were generally accepted, then music would have stepped across a linguistic border, however short the step. As Krenek has put it elsewhere, "We must go back to Monteverdi's time in order to observe a transition from one tonal language to another corresponding to that which took place with Schönberg."[12]

The transition to which Krenek refers in citing Monteverdi is, of course, the transition from modal polyphony to tonal harmony. This is the transition separating the two great distinctive periods of European music, i.e. the modal epoch and the harmonic epoch. None of the many changes that occurred in the course of either of these epochs could compare in significance with the cataclysm at the end of the sixteenth century when the modes gave way before the diatonic scale and opened the way to the tonal, or harmonic era. It is, as we have seen, the latter era that has produced the whole literature familiar to us as classical or serious music.

Today the music lover may listen to and even derive pleasure from the contrapuntal masterpieces of the polyphonic epoch, but he cannot hear them as they were heard in their own time, since he approaches them with certain habits of listening derived from his exclusive association with tonal rather than modal music. He cannot accept a modal term of reference. As in listening to oriental music, he is impressed, not by what impresses its own listeners, but by the manner in which it represents a deviation from the music to which he is accustomed. He is like a Berliner listening to the Dutch language or an Alpine Germanic dialect.

This explains Krenek's device in comparing the neo-classical composers with hypothetical composers of the seventeenth century, "confused by Monteverdi's innovations, going back to the modal style of Palestrina". What he is saying is that atonality is to tonality what tonality was to modality, or tonal harmony to modal polyphony. The neo-classicists, he tells us, do not recognize the new atonal language, or at least do not feel at home in it, and seek refuge in the old language of tonality.

It is also a perceptive and articulate definition of the real meaning of neo-classicism, and Krenek's reference to its "fatal reactionary flavour" can hardly be regarded either as impertinent or overdrawn. Its pertinence is confirmed by the neo-classicists themselves. Theodore Stravinsky, the composer's son, has unwittingly given the game away in his analysis of his father's neo-classicism; an analysis, by the way, that enjoys his father's written endorsement. He says, for instance, in *Le message d'Igor Stravinsky*:

"When Stravinsky 'looks back' or 'returns' to something, then it is to a great fundamental dogma which in the course of an entire romantic century has been almost completely forgotten—to pure music, to music as an absolute art. . . . But if his musical credo embraces the oldest tradition, still it does so with the essential difference that that which with the old masters was spontaneous (and doubtless usually unconscious) is with Stravinsky fully conscious, considered, and reasoned. . . . Whether one finds this a reason for rejoicing or lamentation, this is today a firm fact that can no longer be denied or evaded. . . . This conscious awareness is one of the most significant factors in the musical history of our culture."[13]

And it explains why so many of these composers have

never reached, in their reasoned effort to achieve simplicity, anything like the quality and the popularity attained in their earlier works, which were written more complexly but also more spontaneously. Of this, Stravinsky, Ravel and Richard Strauss are examples.

Krenek touches on this when he notes that "this reaction is distinguished from similar processes in the past primarily by the fact that it was not introduced by a new generation of composers but rather by the leading composers of an established generation." He might better have noted that it was not, indeed, a popular reaction, but rather a tactical reversal of the field by composers whose relationship to the public had become tenuous and whose intellectual instincts and predilections prompted them to look backwards instead of around them. Confronted by Honegger's "wall of accumulated materials", they turned tail.

But the overall validity of Krenek's argument depends upon whether or not atonality is, indeed, a new musical language. That it is intended as a new language need not be questioned, nor the assumption that, if it is a language, it is a new one. The basic questions remain: Is atonality a musical language? If it is a language, has it any other than an academic future?

The answer to the first question would seem to be that atonality is probably a language in the sense that those who devised it also employ it, and even seem to understand it. It is also a language in the sense that it is recognized as such even by composers who do not employ it. If musical evolution is in the hands of the composers, then the linguistic crisis is real and the twelve-tonists are writing the new dictionaries and determining the appropriate syntax.

The answer to the second question, however, whether it

has any future, is a different matter. Real languages are not made. They evolve from the compulsion of people to communicate with one another, and their characteristics are determined by the circumstances of the communities in which they evolve. Scholars may codify them and set general standards of vocabulary, grammar, and syntax, but they cannot invent them. At least, they cannot make an invented language stick. Of this Esperanto is a pertinent example.

Krenek may correctly note the "fatal reactionary flavour" of neo-classical music, but as a twelve-tonist he overlooks the fatal academic flavour of a new musical language without popular roots. The final test of a language is: Do people use it? Applied to music this test emerges: Is it a people's music? Exposed to this test, atonality collapses.

In other words, the interpretation of the present crisis of musical evolution as a linguistic crisis is valid only to those who think of evolution as the exclusive responsibility of serious composers. If this were the case, then one would have to acknowledge the atonalists as the standard-bearers of progress. But the absence of popular origins in their new musical language, and the inability and disinclination of the musical community to adopt it, indicate that this is not the path of musical evolution and that atonality is, in fact, a still-born language.

The only serious composer who has combined insight with the courage to face the facts and draw the consequences is the German, Carl Orff. He has recognized the obsolescence both of the harmonic system and of the symphony orchestra as well as the obsolescence of the classical forms, and has thrown the whole apparatus overboard, reverting to the simplest melodic, rhythmic, and harmonic formulas. The reaction of his contemporaries, both composers and

critics, has been to regard him as a non-musician. In a sense
they are right. It is a matter of definition. If one finds Berg,
Webern, Hindemith, etc., musical, then it is certainly
consistent to find that Orff is no musician.

But even Orff cannot escape sociology. His compositions
may reveal a more profound critical and historical understanding of the contemporary musical situation than the
music of his contemporaries. His impulse to get back to the
basic elements of melody and rhythm is certainly correct.
But his compositions, like those of his contemporaries, also
represent a critical rather than a spontaneously popular
creative accomplishment.

Such works as *Antigone* and even the more easily assimilable *Trionfi*, are admirable in their avoidance of the technical
delusions that beset every other contemporary composer,
and delightful in the drastic manner in which they defy the
instrumental and harmonic conventions hitherto accepted as
indispensable to serious music. But they have no social roots.

Orff, too, is inhibited by the assumption of the inevitability of an art-music separate and distinct from popular
music. He has seen his colleagues stumped by the "wall of
accumulated materials" and has understood the futility of
their exploratory enterprises. He has recognized the necessity for radical measures. And he has done the only thing
that he as a serious composer could do. He has gone back
to primitive elements, to the Middle Ages, to the Greeks,
and to Africa and the Orient.

This is preferable to the compromise retreat of the neo-
classicists to the eighteenth century, or to the esoteric
adventures of the twelve-tonists in atonality, but it collapses
in the face of the fact that the crisis of evolution is not
susceptible of intellectual solution.

The neo-classicist, at least, offers the serious musical audience something related to what it has previously heard, however inferior. The listener finds himself on fairly solid ground, if surrounded by a forbidding landscape. The atonalist, on the other hand, provides him with no point of reference, even within the framework of a single composition, since repetition is a heresy in the dogma of atonalism. And an Orff, except in the relatively popular *Carmina Burana*, gives only an intellectually distilled primitiveness with which the audience has little in common.

Whatever the method, the composer's claim to historical continuity is supportable only on paper. The listener does not feel his product as music. As long as this is the case, its claim to being music at all is dubious. As Hindemith has said "A musical structure which, due to its extreme novelty, does not, in the listener's mind, summon up any recollections of former experiences, or which incessantly disappoints his constructive expectations, will prevent his creative co-operation."[10]

The contemporary composer is, in short, caught between two fires, with all exits blocked. As a serious composer he is committed to the composition of music to which meaning can be attributed, or which is at least sufficiently extensive in form to warrant a claim to significance. It is also required of his music that it be original: that it support the assumption that music is still an art in progress. But harmony, without which neither the illusion of meaning nor the actuality of large forms in the traditional sense is possible, can no longer be used in a manner at once effective and original. The existing devices cannot be used originally, and original devices are ineffective.

The composer persists in his search for the harmonic

solution of his creative troubles. His chances of discovering anything worth the trouble are slim. It's more than looking for a needle in a haystack. All rational examination of the circumstances indicates that in this haystack there is no needle.

II

## MELODY

Why, one may ask, does the contemporary composer not go back to simple monodic melody?

One would be tempted to answer simply: because the evolutionary crisis of western music is a crisis of harmony, not of melody.

But it is not as simple as that. Harmony is, to be sure, the root crisis. But it has bred others, including a melodic crisis, and an examination of them is essential if we are to get the basic harmonic crisis into focus and attempt to understand what happened to serious music.

The best place to study the melodic crisis is in the theatre. The European music that we all know and love was born there (at the beginning of the seventeenth century) from a desire to reconstitute the function of vocal melody as the lyrical extension of a poetic text. Before the century was out the expressive associations of the cadences, figures, ornaments and "affections" of the new vocal idiom were so generally accepted and understood that they remained effective without a text and could provide the melodic basis for purely instrumental music. It is in the theatre, and only there, that we can hope to solve the mystery of how a music, born of a melodic rebellion against the sterile complexity of modal polyphony, should have arrived at its present state of melodic sterility.

The story of European music, or that phase of it from which the standard repertoire is drawn, begins with the rediscovery in the Italian theatre of an essentially monodic music, with chordal accompaniment added as a souvenir of the polyphonic tradition and as an accommodation to ears accustomed to a multiplicity of voices. In that chordal accompaniment lay the dramatic, dynamic and graphic elements which, for three centuries, were to provide the materials for the most glorious achievements of European music—and for the ultimate catastrophe which we have been experiencing in this century.

If one thinks of the greatest glories of European music, one is likely to think first of symphonies and instrumental chamber music rather than operas; for the musical instrument, particularly the collective instrument of the orchestra, has usually been the European composer's most congenial and fruitful medium. In view of this it may seem perverse to concentrate on opera rather than on the concert hall in studying the factors and factions which determined the course of European musical evolution. It should suffice, however, to reiterate that this music was born in the theatre, that the orchestra and the forms of later instrumental music all originated there, that almost all the great instrumental composers wrote for the theatre, and that Wagner, the man who exposed the outer limits of chromatic harmony and brought the orchestra to its most sumptuous estate, wrote for nothing else.

The theatrical works of Monteverdi, Alessandro Scar-latti, Handel, Gluck, Mozart, Cimarosa, Beethoven, Cherubini, Spontini, Rossini, Meyerbeer, Weber, Donizetti,

Bellini, Verdi, Gounod, Massenet, Wagner, Mascagni, Puccini, Strauss, Debussy and Berg provide all that we need to describe the arc of European music's rise and fall. The arc has been sustained by tensions arising from the conflicting claims of melody and harmony, of singer and orchestra, and of song and a music that would be more than song.

Curiously, but not insignificantly, the singer himself remained without influence. At each step along the way he had to yield to the overriding demands of the orchestra and a harmonic concept of musical expression. He had his moments, to be sure. There were times when the singer ruled the roost and composers did his bidding. But the trend of evolution was against him. History records these as bad periods. They were terminated by reform movements initiated by Gluck and Wagner and born of the conviction that there was more to music than mere song or mere singers could provide.

The "more" was always found in harmony, and the instrument of harmony was the orchestra, whose wealth of dynamic and graphic resources, as developed by successive generations of imaginative and daring composers, could offer more than the voice, or even mixed voices, towards the fulfilment of harmony's dramatic implications. The singer was doomed, along with his song. Only a very few, Hanslick among them, could foresee that the orchestra's victory would be pyrrhic; that with its harmonic sustenance exhausted by the struggle, there could be nothing new for it to sing, and that even the objective of song would be forgotten.

The nature of the conflict and its implications were never understood, even by the contestants. The reform composers did not realize that in favouring the orchestra they were imposing upon it vocal responsibilities. And the singers who acquiesced in the surrender of their primacy, themselves fascinated by the orchestra and the challenge of orchestral participation, failed to notice that what was at stake was the very life-blood of music: vocal melody.

Nor were these implications apparent to the public. Opera-lovers have always favoured what are known as singers' operas, but they are little disposed to challenge the historical judgment of *Otello* and *Falstaff* as superior to *Rigoletto*, *Il Trovatore* and *Traviata*, or of *Tristan und Isolde* as superior to *Tannhäuser* and *The Flying Dutchman*. Our musical society goes no farther than to note that up to the time of *Der Rosenkavalier* opera was a living art and that since then it has not been. It would never think to seek in Wagner, Verdi and Strauss the root of the evil, least of all to look for it in what are admittedly their finest works.

The most spectacular, if by no means the only villain of the piece is Wagner. Modern opera, like most modern music, is reactionary, and no other composer is so stigmatized by the reaction as Wagner. The length of his operas, his system of leit-motifs, the size and richness of his orchestra, the fullness of his harmonies, the ecstasies of his progressions, the philosophical pretensions of his poems—all are rejected. But these have to do with manner rather than with method. Wagner's method—the integration of music and drama, with music subordinate to the text—has survived. The irony of this is that no composer has ever so flagrantly and successfully violated his own proclaimed method. Wagner's music has survived, not because of his method, but in spite of it.

The simple fact is that people go to Wagnerian music-dramas to hear the music—in the orchestra and on the stage.

They go to hear "The Ride of the Valkyries", the "Wald-weben", "Wotan's Farewell", "The Magic Fire Music", "Winterstuerme", "Du bist der Lenz", Siegfried's "Funeral March" and "Rhine Journey", Bruennhilde's "Immola-tion", Walther's "Prize Song", Isolde's "Liebestod"—and so on—all musical episodes of lyric, epic and sometimes even dramatic grandeur, and all distinguished by great melodic invention.

The musical basis of Wagner's popularity escaped his successors. They held to his method and discarded his manner, not recognizing that what was valid and vital in Wagner was precisely his manner, including particularly the excesses and extravagances which the contemporary com-poser so heartily despises and which the contemporary lay listener still so passionately admires.

Composers interpreted the method as directed not only against the star singer, but also against song. They over-looked the fact that Wagner's orchestra sings. When Wagner inhibited his singers by imposing upon them a vocal line closer to speech than to song, he saw to it that the melodic loss was made good in the orchestra—and so did Verdi and Strauss. Later composers simply observed the absence of set vocal pieces, and concluded that Wagner, Verdi and Strauss had evolved something better. They hadn't.

Wagner was always a musician, a musical composer in spite of himself. He achieved success and immortality in the theatre just as Bellini, Mozart, Rossini, Donizetti, Meyer-beer and Verdi did—by writing great melodies. He was music's greatest unwitting hypocrite. He was determined to bridle the singer, but instinctively he realized the telling effect of a high note forcefully delivered as the climax of a long melodic line. And Wagnerian opera today is dominated by the tenor and the prima donna just as any other opera is; indeed, even more so since so few singers meet the requirements. And Wagner compounded the paradox by giving the orchestra responsibilities that it can fulfil only under the most inspired and authoritative leadership, and established in the person of the conductor a new star.

It is easy to scoff at the contemporary composer for having confused a sterile method with a fruitful manner and for having attempted to practise what Wagner had preached. But he had, in fact, no choice. It was simply impossible to continue much farther in the direction pointed by Wagner's manner. There had to be a limit to loudness and richness and bigness and reckless modulation. Wagner did not quite reach it. But he came close, and Strauss had no difficulty in finishing the job with the tone poems and with *Salome*, *Elektra* and *Der Rosenkavalier*.

Nor should one forget what must have seemed the hopeful example of Verdi, whose course from *Nabucco* to *Falstaff* was clearly in the direction of the integrated music-drama, but whose mature product was happily free from Wagner's Germanic trappings. It is easy to understand, at this distance, the temptation *Otello* and *Falstaff* represented. They offered more concentrated, more pointed, more modern excitement and pleasure than the conventional grand opera. The pace was faster, the action more direct and, in the case of *Otello*, more violent and shocking. They must have seemed at the time to be a step towards real music-drama, a closer approximation than Wagner had been able to achieve of a complete jelling of the various arts involved in opera.

Such an appreciation was correct enough, but the conclusions drawn from it were as mistaken as those drawn from the similar appreciation of Wagner, and hardly less disastrous, although easier to forgive. Verdi was the more honest progressive of the two, or at least the more consistent, and his results were more convincing. Wagner's visions were a bit ridiculous. Verdi's never were. He had as good a sense of the theatre as Wagner, and a more conscious understanding of the essentially musical nature of opera and the essentially melodic nature of music. Thus it was easy to believe that *Otello* and *Falstaff* owed their success and the high esteem in which they were held to what was new in them rather than to what was old.

This was true as far as the critics and the initiated public were concerned. But it was not the new that kept the operas in the repertoire. It was what still survived of the earlier Verdi. Critics may praise as they will the declamatory style of *Otello*. But what keeps it in the repertoire is the opening chorus, and the "Esultate!", the "Drinking Song", the first act duet, the "Credo", the Iago-Otello duet at the close of the second act, the great choral scene and Otello's monologue at the end of the third act, and Desdemona's arias and Otello's valedictory in the fourth. There are fewer such melodic excursions in *Falstaff*, which is why *Falstaff* is less often in the repertoire than *Otello*.

Hanslick sensed this acutely when he heard *Otello* in Milan in 1887, shortly after the première, and commented:

"Song remains the decisive element, but it follows closely the course of thought, feeling, and word. Independent, self-sufficient, symmetrically constructed melodies appear less frequently than does that cross between recitative and cantilena which now dominates modern opera. . . . If the right choice of colour for every mood and the emphatic notation of every turn of speech were the single objective of opera, then we could unhesitatingly declare *Otello* to be an improvement over *Aida* and Verdi's finest work.

"This devotion to the poem does not, however, release the opera composer from other obligations. He must above all else be a musician, and on this basis we expect music not only in accord with the text but also attractive to us simply as music—individual, original and self-sufficient. . . . We demand of the opera composer beauty and novelty of musical ideas, particularly melodic ideas. And from this point of view *Otello* strikes me as less adequate than *Aida*, *Traviata* or *Un Ballo in Maschera*."[14]

This was sound commentary, but in vain. Thanks to a trend begun by Beethoven and carried to its effective limits by Wagner, "beauty and novelty of musical ideas, particularly melodic ideas", were no longer enough, despite the abundance of such ideas in the music of both Beethoven and Wagner. With the ascendancy of harmonic movement over melodic movement and of the orchestra over the voice, the trend was away from vocal melody and towards illustrative device. It was to lead ultimately to the moving-picture sound-track.

To the succeeding generation it did not appear, as it did to some in the case of Wagner, that Verdi had reached a limit. They reckoned that his was a procedure offering reasonable prospects. This proved to be the case, if in a limited degree. The job of running out the vein, performed for German opera by Strauss and for French opera by Debussy and Charpentier, was done for the Italians by Leoncavallo, Mascagni, Giordano, Cilea and Puccini. It is no mere coincidence that the last really sure-fire aria in the repertoire, "Nessun dorma", from *Turandot*, occurs in the last act of Puccini's last opera.

It was the end of the road, as it had to be when a musical art that had for a hundred years been growing ever less melodic finally ceased to sing at all. For in aspiring to more than song the European composers had denied those very lyric faculties of music that prompt people to express themselves musically and that make the musical expression of others intelligible. Preoccupied with harmony and orchestration, they had forgotten that the musician's primary purpose in life is to sing.

European music collapsed because its technical resources —diatonic and chromatic harmony, primarily, but also certain rhythmic and orchestral devices which shall concern us later—were exhausted; but the collapse was rendered inevitable by the fact that these were essentially secondary or auxiliary resources. By his dependence upon them to the ultimate exclusion of the one inexhaustible resource of vocal melody, the contemporary composer showed that, while he had learned much about the techniques and devices by which the dramatic implications of our harmonic system could be exploited effectively, he had forgotten what music is.

The normal means of communication is speech. All speech is coloured by variations of pitch and rhythm employed spontaneously to supplement the precision or imprecision of words with a sense of the feelings associated with them. Thus all speech is in some degree musical, and all speakers composers, in however rudimentary a way. Verbal communication is never entirely dissociated from musical communication. Musical expression begins when a baby first uses its vocal chords.

Poetry is a musical extension of speech. It is distinguished from speech by a rhythmical organization whose purpose is to encourage, support, and animate a vocal tone more

consciously and more consistently sustained than is customary or practical in speech. The advantage of the sustained
tone of poetry over the unsustained or very much less
sustained tone of speech is its plasticity. The melodic
variation can be enriched and accentuated, and the opportunities for expressive colouration are infinitely increased, if
only because the tone is of longer duration and gives the
speaker more time for its lyrical exploitation.

If one wishes to go beyond the poet's capacities for
sensuous or melodic communication, song is the next step.
Here the voice is fully sustained, and the melodic component
of the communication is dominant, if not exclusive. The
communication is sensuous rather than intellectual, general
rather than precise, but at the same time more precisely
individual, since the singer can substitute for the words that
everybody uses an infinity of lyrical inflections which only he
can use because, since they are personal, only he can invent
them.

Song has the advantage over prose and poetry of an
incomparably greater range of expressive colour and
emphasis, since the sound can be regulated in pitch,
augmented or diminished in volume, and accelerated or
retarded in movement in a purely musical way. Because of
sustained, plastic, malleable sound, music can work in
expressive spheres where prose, bound to the word, and
poetry, released from absolute verbal precision, but still
constrained by a text, cannot go. This is why the poet writes
verse instead of prose, and it is why the musician should
work with song rather than with verse.

The evolutionary course of music since Beethoven's time
has been in the opposite direction. Musicians have acted as
though music's intellectual imprecision were a fault, and as

though its salvation lay in finding in music the narrative and descriptive faculties which are the natural attributes of speech, poetry, painting, and sculpture. This was because the picturesque and dramatic implications of harmony and the orchestra led them to assume that music's ultimate objectives were dramatic and picturesque. Instead of making opera the extension of the theatre in song, as Mozart did, composers since Wagner's and Verdi's time have tended to make it a theatrical extension of music. They have behaved as if song were something to be ashamed of—and have produced a songless music of which they should be ashamed.

Parlando recitative or dry declamation has replaced the aria and the concerted piece. Choral commentary has replaced the exuberant song of massed voices. Ballet has disappeared, by which opera has been deprived, not only of song, but of dance. Even the orchestra, opera's last great singer, has become a humble provider of commas, full-stops, exclamation marks, descriptive colour, inflated dynamic contrasts, and mood-painting. The faculties of free, emotional, sensuous expression in song, which are music's purest and most utterly native property, have been denied, as if composers were all ascetics, and song a cardinal sin.

It is in the opera house that the ascetic character of modern music is most keenly felt. A symphony without song may deceive by its thematic workmanship and the skill and ingenuity of its orchestration. In the opera house, with attention diverted from the orchestra to the stage, the absence of song is insupportable. For there is less music in the declamation of modern opera than in the spoken lines of the modern theatre.

The kind of declamation or parlando recitative now fashionable in modern opera defeats rather than assists the musical objective. By restricting the voice to arbitrary pitches in a manner incompatible with the melodic-structural character of both speech and song, the composer puts the singer in a melodic-emotional strait-jacket. The vocal line to which he is constrained offers less opportunity for melodic expression than the flattest sort of prose. Nothing has been written in the opera since *Turandot* that could compare as music with any Shakespearian speech, even when delivered by a third-rate actor.

It is not because it is no longer possible to write melodies within the existing scale system. Original and effective melodies are being written every day, and the United States, during precisely the period covered by what we call modern music, has experienced a kind of golden age of melody, thanks to such fertile melodists as Jerome Kern, George Gershwin, Irving Berlin, Richard Rodgers, Cole Porter, and many, many others. The melodic resources of our scales are by no means exhausted. It is rather that the kind of melody listeners like to hear is no longer integral to the late traditions of European music.

It was possible for Mozart, Rossini, Weber, Donizetti, Bellini and Verdi to write arias that were just as much song hits as "Star Dust", "Summertime", and "Some Enchanted Evening", and which achieved on barrel-organs and in every conceivable orchestra, band, and piano arrangement, a dissemination corresponding to that accomplished for hit tunes today by the radio, the gramophone, and the juke-box. But first Beethoven and then Wagner taught the sophisticated music lover to regard such music as trivial, or at least incompatible with the concept of music's higher responsibilities in the field of philosophical and psychological articulation.

Modern opera reveals the full calamity of serious music, both in the theatre and in the concert hall. An art that originated as the creative extension of the rudimentary music of speech has ended, in the more radical of its present forms, by being less musical than the gurgle of a newborn babe. For fifty years composers have been giving us recitative and parlando operas that disdain the agreeable, sensuous communication of song, vocal or instrumental, without substituting for it the precise articulation of the spoken word. They have given us operas which, uncommunicative musically, are dependent for communication upon an almost prosaic rendering of the text. The singer is restricted to declamation in order that the text may be understood, and then is drowned out by a clamorous orchestra in order that the composer may still claim to have written an opera.

If we extend our study to purely instrumental music we get substantially the same picture, except that the composer is the worse off for the absence of the visual aid and diversion of the stage. What distinguishes opera as we know it from any kind of musical theatre is precisely what distinguishes the whole body of European music from any other music, namely, the harmonic exploitation of our major and minor scales. The composer of purely instrumental music, or purely choral music, is, like the composer for the theatre, condemned by tradition and by the traditional use of his resources to the production of music with dramatic and thoughtful implications. He is also expected to be original. From Beethoven's time to the present the evolutionary trend has been towards an increasingly prosaic objective. Until recently the composer could compensate for and cover up the lyrical loss by striking originality in the exploitation of his harmonic and instrumental resources. Now he can no longer be original within the required harmonic frame of reference. His failure exposes a shattering dénouement in which we learn that a music that aspired to be more than song can no longer sing.


III

RHYTHM


The only musical element that may be said to have rivalled harmony in the contemporary composer's technical preoccupations is rhythm.

Although this is not apparent in the excellent studies of the problems of contemporary music by such thoughtful composers as Schönberg, Krenek, Stravinsky, Hindemith, Honegger, Sessions and Copland, who discuss harmony at length and rhythm only briefly, if at all, it is apparent in their compositions, where rhythmic speculation and experiment are almost as common as unresolved dissonance.

Of the basic musical elements—melody, harmony and rhythm—the latter has been the least highly developed and the least systematically exploited in European music, which suffers conspicuously in this respect by comparison with African and oriental musical systems. This is not to say that it has not played an important role. It is rather that the rhythmic characteristics of European music have been determined by considerations in which rhythm either was not the primary factor or was not recognized as such. While the European masters devoted intensive study to the development of harmony and orchestration, there is little evidence of a corresponding academic concern with rhythm. The rhythmic characteristics of European music seem rather to have followed naturally and inevitably from harmonic and instrumental evolution.

This may seem strange at first glance to those who have struggled as musical amateurs with the problems of counting beats and bars, and calculating the time values of dotted notes. Nor would it seem to fit in with the size of the battery in the modern symphony orchestra, nor with the fact that European music's most important personage has been for many years a man whose basic function is to beat time. And, indeed, it is true that these phenomena do reflect a concern with rhythmic problems. But they also reflect the absence of the organic pulsation common to other musical systems, usually provided by drums or other percussion instruments from within the instrumental body and from within the fabric of musical composition, whether written out or improvised.

Indeed, the nearest thing to a rhythm-generating instrument the European orchestra has ever had was the harpsichord, which, under the hands of the Kapellmeister (frequently the composer himself), was used until the end of the eighteenth century much as the piano is used today in the direction of an instrumental ensemble by Duke Ellington and Count Basie. In European music the percussion instruments have never otherwise been the pace setters. They have tended to be an adjunct of instrumentation rather than a generator of pulsation. The pace and the pulse have always been set and governed by a conductor. One hastens to add that long before he became the interpretive virtuoso of the baton familiar to audiences today, the conductor existed in European music, either as the man at the harpsichord, as the leader of the violins, or as the firm and frequently audible *batteur de mesure*.

Comparing the European with other musical systems, it is easy to cite the need for a conductor as evidence of rhythmic debility, as, indeed, it is. But the rhythmic peculiarities of European music cannot be dismissed so casually, nor so casually condemned; for the absence of a dominant pulsation, by removing the constraint of adherence to an inevitable beat, has also made possible a rhythmic freedom without which European music could not have achieved its greatest reflective, dramatic and illustrative attributes. It is, thus, not really a question of rhythmic debility but rather of rhythmic ambiguity, derived from the fact that European music is an instrumental art shaped by a vocal art, and that the symphony orchestra, that grandest and most characteristic instrument of European music, entered upon the scene as a humble auxiliary in a theatre dominated by singers.

When vocal polyphony gave way to accompanied vocal monody in the Italian theatre at the beginning of the seventeenth century, the instrumental ensemble took its place in the pit as a derivative of the dance-band. Most of the secular instrumental music of the time was confined to popular dance forms, or was derived from them, and was influenced rhythmically accordingly. But in the first century and a half of the new European music the singer was dominant, and the singer's approach to rhythm, particularly the Italian singer's, is notoriously less inhibited than the instrumentalist's. A clash between the two attitudes could be postponed as long as the orchestra was responsible for accompaniment and the provision of such *divertissements* as the overtures and interludes which were to ripen ultimately into the three-movement symphonies of Haydn and Mozart. But when it began to be more widely employed as

THE COMPOSER AND HIS MATERIALS

a participant in the singer's dramatic and lyrical enterprise, conflict became inevitable.

It has never been finally resolved. Indeed, it has hardly been recognized, much less generally understood. It has rather been sensed, or felt; and reaction to it has been instinctive and tentative rather than calculated. Many of our conventions, both of composition and of execution, derive from a kind of empirical accommodation rather than any attempt at negotiated resolution.

The initial compromise was the device of recitative, a concession to the singer's need for opportunities to exploit the expressive faculties of declamation uninhibited by instrumental intrusion and the rhythmic dictation of a time-beater. The recitative made it possible within the framework of an episode dominated by the instrumental concept of rhythm to set off areas in which rhythmic refinements were left to a soloist's discretion. This demanded adjustments from singer and orchestra alike, but it left both with fixed and mutually respected opportunities for the unrestricted exercise of their respective rhythmic predilections.

It was satisfactory as long as instrumental music retained its purely instrumental character. It survived the full bloom of the orchestra as the dominant and representative execu-tant of European music in the mature works of Haydn and Mozart. Solo instruments even adopted recitative, and singers learned to adjust to the instrumental approach where the equal participation of voice and instruments made precision mandatory.

But from Beethoven's time on composers tended to re-quire of the orchestra itself something approaching a vocal type of expression. The purpose of instrumental music was conceived more and more in terms of meaning than

c

movement. The rhythmic element, in the sense of a pattern of sustained pulsation in which performer and listener could participate equally, and with equal assurance that their rhythmic expectations would not be betrayed, receded into the background. Without systematizing the recitative formula, composers gave to instrumental music an increasingly expressive, dramatic or, if you will, recitative character. A musical art in which instrumental music and an instrumental approach to rhythm had achieved dominance now began to find its destiny in a vocal concept of musical expression. With the change of emphasis in performance from self-evident execution to speculative interpretation, both composer and listener began to look for more sophisticated sources of dynamic movement than the insistent pulse of an established beat.

Historically this seemed to represent a swing back to the vocal concept of rhythm, to the plastic melodic phrase moulded expressively by a singer employing free rhythmic devices derived from speech and poetry to make the phrase articulate. But it occurred in an art whose instrumental character was already established, and which was already burdened with a numerous ensemble. The execution of music conceived rhapsodically and tending to a vocal concept of rhythm could not be left to the discretion of fifty or sixty individuals, each with his own interpretive ideas and convictions. The vocal and instrumental concepts of rhythm were in conflict again, but the new problem was to reconcile, not only the difference between singer and orchestra, but also the differences between one player in the orchestra and another. An arbiter was needed.

Even in the seventeenth and eighteenth centuries there had always been, as we have noted, somebody in charge—a man at the harpsichord, the concert-master with his bow, or a *batteur de mesure* with a roll of parchment or a stick. But his had been a co-ordinating and supervisory rather than an interpretive and executive function. When the instrumental concept of rhythm was in the ascendancy, the pulse of a firm rhythm was felt and respected, and, once set in motion, it was sustained throughout a movement. As long as this was the case it was no great task to keep an ensemble tolerably together, although European music never had the rhythmic inevitability of African or oriental systems, or even of jazz, whose larger ensembles achieve without a conductor (in the modern symphonic sense) a precision matched in symphonic music even today only by the finest orchestras under conductors of the first class.

At the beginning of the nineteenth century, however, the steady pulse, explicit or implicit, was compromised in favour of other and apparently nobler considerations, and a strong interpretive and executive hand was required to make good the loss. Somebody had to stand up and take charge, to be responsible, not only for the beat, but also for controlled deviations from the beat, not only for co-ordination, but also for interpretation. These were responsibilities that could not be shared with those of the harpsichordist (or pianist) or first violinist. The new conductor had to be that and nothing else. He was found in the person of the man with a baton who has imposed his will upon orchestras, singers and, to some extent, upon audiences ever since. By the end of the second decade of the century he was an established institution.

Through him it was possible to achieve a rhythmic flexibility combined with precision that would have been impossible had the individual members of the orchestra and the individual singers been left to their own devices. Under a good conductor it was now vouchsafed to the orchestra to achieve a plastic line previously accessible only to the singer or, occasionally, to an instrumental soloist working in a vocal style. To over-simplify, it was the conductor's contribution to make the orchestra sing.

It has also been, as we shall see, to discourage and inhibit the inner pulse which is as much an element of music's life-blood as vocal melody. In other musical systems such preoccupation with the business of keeping time as betrayed by the visible counting of the conductor and the invisible counting of the players and singers would seem preposterous. In other systems the beat is there, and is felt as a sovereign pulse by player and listener alike. But they are not similarly burdened—or blessed—with such uniquely European complications as harmony and counterpoint, which often require that the horizontal impulses of the beat be compromised in favour of the vertical impulses of multiple-voiced composition achieved through harmonic progression.

Of all elements of music, rhythm is the most difficult to discuss, if only because it is so difficult to define. To draw the line between melody and rhythm, for instance, is impossible, since melody, in more than the purely detached sense of a series of higher and lower pitches, cannot exist without some sort of ordered movement. Even harmony, through its dynamic properties, can have a rhythmic function. The movement from tonic to dominant and dominant to tonic is almost certain, unless artificially frustrated, to develop a rhythmic momentum.

However, for the purpose of this discussion, which is to seek insight into the contemporary composer's problems, it may suffice to accept rhythm as referring to that element of music that has to do with movement, the functions of movement and the government of movement. Since the composer's problems arise from the abuse of his inherited materials, rhythm no less than harmony, the problems can be understood only in terms of what has happened to the materials.

In the case of rhythm this can best be studied by comparing familiar compositions from contrasted phases of European music, with an eye to their characteristics of movement. Let us compare, for instance, a Brandenburg Concerto with a tone poem by Strauss; *The Marriage of Figaro* with *Tristan und Isolde*; a symphony by Mozart or Haydn with a symphony by Bruckner or Mahler. Several rhythmic facts are immediately apparent. The earlier pieces move more easily and more spontaneously. They are less dependent upon the urge to move communicated and regulated by a conductor. The pulsation seems to originate in the music itself. One has the feeling that an orchestra, given the beat, could carry on without further prodding, guidance or control. With the later works one feels that the orchestra, without the conductor, would not make much progress.

There are other than rhythmic reasons for this. As the nineteenth century drew to a close, the richness of the harmonic idiom and the obesity of the modern orchestra tended to inhibit horizontal movement. Music moved less easily simply because there was more of it to move. And movement became less essential as the dynamic substance in the vertical phenomenon of the chord superseded the horizontal dynamics of the rhythmic pattern.

But there were rhythmic reasons, too. One feels in the

later music that the objective is more plastic, that what counts is not the structure growing naturally out of a self-evident blend of rhythmic melodic and harmonic factors, but rather a design moulded by the conductor from an accumulation of rhythmic, melodic and harmonic elements left at his disposal for the accomplishment of the composer's expressive purpose. This is closer to the vocal concept of rhythm. It shows us the conductor, not only as the man who makes the orchestra sing, but also as the supreme singer of European music.

Another way of understanding this is simply to look at the scores. The older ones are innocent of expression marks, the later ones full of them. The inference is that in the older works the sheerly structural problem was solved in the printed score. Assuming a reasonably just tempo, the harmonic and melodic structural elements cannot help but assert themselves. They are present in such a way that a person of adequate technical competence and normal musicianship cannot escape their implications.

The significance of this in a consideration of rhythm is the fact that, once an older piece is set in motion, architecture takes place almost automatically. The structural elements are all present, properly assorted and measured. With no more than the establishment of a pace they begin to fall easily and inevitably into place. To put it even more simply, the form is ready-made. It needs only the rhythmic pulse to give it life.

This has been true of very little serious music since Beethoven's time, and it is certainly not true of much that has been regarded as the greatest. The change is accountable only in part to the general trend towards a harmonically vertical rather than a melodically linear kind of dynamism.

The trend existed, to be sure, but it was not the only source of new dynamic effects, nor even the most important. Along with the dynamism yielded by unexpected chords and modulations came a rhythmic dynamism yielded, not by momentum, but by its interruption.

This is the essence of recitative which in its simplest form merely permits the singer to be rhythmically free. He uses this freedom not just to escape the tedium of counting time, nor to abandon rhythm altogether, but rather to alter the rhythmic pulse, or cheat it, for expressive effect. It is a device of dynamics, and it gains its dynamic effects by keeping the listener in doubt as to what the pulsation is to be, by anticipating or disappointing his rhythmic expectations.

Anyone who has been subjected to the unexpected braking of a motor car or a lift, or has been suddenly precipitated into motion at an unwonted speed, has learned how exciting an unanticipated rhythmic deviation can be. This is the rhythmic significance of the *accelerandi, allargandi, morendi, ritardandi, rubati, fermate, a tempi,* etc., in which the scores of the nineteenth century abound. They all refer to the interruption, alteration or restoration of an established rhythm.

Thus, just as the composers of the nineteenth century excited their listeners with new and daring harmonies, so also did they excite them with deviations from the accepted patterns of movement. They exposed them to propulsion, retardation, sudden changes of pace, abrupt starts and stops, etc. These devices all served expressive purposes and contributed to the listener's sense of dramatic occurrence and adventurous exploration. But they were also devices to which listeners could become accustomed, and, as with the devices of modulation, there was a limit to their extension.

In other words, what the nineteenth-century composers did to tonal harmony they also did to rhythm. An approach to rhythm based on the contradiction rather than the accommodation of the listener's expectations led to a situation where this rhythmic feeling was unresponsive to further abuse. The listener who found any harmony tolerable, if not necessarily pleasurable, reacted with the same indifference to any new rhythmic deviation. The composer was again faced with an abused resource whose further exploitation within the framework of the serious composer's expressive purpose and traditional methods and techniques offered no reasonable prospects of profit.

The simple solution would have been to return to a simple, steady beat, easily recognized and participated in by the listener. This is still possible, just as simple melody and simple harmony are still possible. It is not that the listener has lost his capacity to find pleasure in a simple melody, a simple harmony, or a simple rhythm. It is rather that he has lost the capacity to be much affected by deviations from simplicity. The composer, on the other hand, must deviate in order to be original and "serious". Thus the straightforward solution of his rhythmic problem is as impossible as the melodic solution to his harmonic problem. He would find himself writing popular music instead of the emotionally, dramatically, intellectually and graphically extraordinary music expected of him as a serious composer.

The situation has not always appeared so hopeless. In the early decades of our century composers already becoming aware of the harmonic dead-end, and rebelling against the German intellectual pretentiousness that had brought them to it, did, for a time, and with some success, look for a solution in a return to an instrumental concept of rhythm. They turned to ballet, and in such fine works as *The Firebird*, *Petrouchka*, *Le Sacré du Printemps*, *Daphnis and Chloe*, *La Valse*, *The Three Cornered Hat*, *The Amazing Mandarin*, *Pas d'Acier* and many others, including such recent examples as Boris Blacher's *Hamlet* and Werner Egk's *Abraxas* they produced the century's most notable and successful music. But this proved, in the long run, to be an unsatisfactory compromise. The composer cannot fulfil his assumed responsibilities as a writer of serious music simply by composing ballets. The proper setting for his music is the concert hall or the opera house, and his proper audience is one which comes, not to look, but to listen.

Faced with his own predilection for the instrumental concept of rhythm and the traditional requirement that he avoid the obvious, the composer has more recently come up with a new compromise. It pleases nobody, but it at least preserves the reputation for complexity essential to the superstitition that the serious composer is somehow superior to the simple fellows who write pleasant music. He writes, instead, a pulsative music but in a sophisticated way. He rejects the four-beats-to-the-bar, four-bars-to-the-phrase type of rhythmical symmetry that is the dance music basis of European instrumental music. To accept it, as long as he chooses to emphasize rhythm, would bring him close to conformity in the popular sense and to triviality in the serious sense. He chooses to regard this symmetry as the "tyranny of the bar line" and to defy it accordingly.

This breaking of the bar line has been matched in futility only by the composer's efforts to break the bonds of tonality by evolving an atonal system. In both cases the composer has got himself into a fix where he is more dependent than ever upon just those technical elements from which he sought emancipation. No composers have been so hamstrung by problems of harmony as the atonalists, and no composers have been so tortured by the problems of rhythm as those who broke the bar line.

It is not, so far as rhythm is concerned, that the bar line might not well be broken. It is an artificial device. The important thing in rhythm is not the symmetrical pattern, of which the bar line is a symbol, but the establishment of a pulse. The symmetrical pattern is of melodic rather than rhythmic origin. And the bar line is a convenience in keeping track of melodic rather than rhythmic progress.

Indeed, the composer's revolt was not so much against the bar line itself as against the regularity of its occurrence. Thus, in place of the traditional adherence to consecutive bars, each bar with the same number of beats, he experimented with a kind of rhythm in which the number of beats to the bar was constantly changed.

His purpose was to emphasize the rhythmic character and content of his music by providing greater rhythmic variety. To put it in terms of the historical perspective, he attempted to replace the variety inherent in the vocal concept of rhythm, but dependent upon the performer for realization at the performer's discretion, with a variety determined and worked out by the composer, leaving nothing to the performer but the job of counting beats and bars.

His accomplishment was to deprive his music of rhythmic inevitability and intelligibility. The harmonic catastrophe was duplicated by a rhythmic catastrophe. By denying the listener a tonal frame of reference, the effort to free music of tonality left the listener incapable of harmonic participation. Similarly, the effort to free rhythm from the constraints of easily recognized patterns deprived the listener of a rhythmic frame of reference and rendered his rhythmic participation impossible.

Here again we have confirmation from the thoughtful Honegger.

"I myself," he writes, "remain very sceptical about these rhythmic refinements. They have no significance except on paper. They are not felt by the listener. . . . After a performance of Stravinsky's *Symphony in C* the players in the orchestra all remarked 'One has no time to listen or appraise. One is too busy counting quavers'. Dependence upon the metronome robs the composer and the interpreter of any freedom. . . . What counts today is rhythmic shock, not melodic beauty."[2]

Honegger forgot to add that even shock is no longer effective. The audience is as numbed rhythmically as it is numbed harmonically. But the truth of what he says about the interpreter must be readily acknowledged by any layman who has watched a virtuoso conduct a Brahms symphony and then watched the same man conduct a modern work. The Brahms will have been largely a choreographic performance, the movement of the hands, arms, and body communicating not only the beat but also the conductor's interpretation of the music being played. It is the conductor's way of being a singer. In the modern composition he will have been preoccupied almost exclusively with the problem of beating time and giving entrances. In short, if the romantics made of the conductor a supreme singer, the moderns seem bent on turning him into a metronome.

For the listener to participate in this music would require that he become a metronome, too. To expect him to do so is unrealistic.

IV

# THE ORCHESTRA

While one is accustomed to think of melody, harmony and rhythm as the basic elements of music, orchestration is so integral a part of the concept and process of composition in the work of the European masters, particularly the later ones, that a discussion of the composer's materials can hardly be complete without adding the orchestra as a fourth element.

It is the instrument for which the symphonies of Haydn, Mozart, Beethoven, Schubert, Mendelssohn, Schumann, Brahms, Tchaikovsky, Bruckner and Mahler were written. Without it the tone poems of Berlioz, Liszt and Strauss, the tone paintings of Debussy and Ravel, the music-dramas of Wagner and the later operas of Verdi would be unthinkable.

It is the executive glory of European music and, next to harmony, its most distinctive phenomenon. What sets it apart from the instrumental ensembles of other musical systems is its function as an instrumental substitute for multiple-voiced song. Its growth and ultimate form were shaped by requirements originating in the multiple-voiced character of the European harmonic system.

Although one may think of harmony and orchestration separately, and study them as only distantly related techniques, they are, in fact, inseparable. Every step in the evolution of harmony from the seventeenth century to the twentieth has been executed either by the orchestra or by a substitute for it—that is, by a smaller combination of orchestral instruments or by a keyboard instrument. Since Beethoven's time, harmonic evolution has been, to a great extent, not only orchestrally executed, but also orchestrally conceived.

Combined with harmony, the symphony orchestra provided apparently inexhaustible resources of colour, dynamics, rhythmic emphases, harmonic fulfilment and sonority. The fascination exercised upon the growing bourgeois audience of the nineteenth century by exciting harmonic experiment with chords, harmonic progressions, and modulation has been intensified through the resources of the orchestra. The suggestive faculties of novel harmonic combinations when played on the piano were nothing compared with the suggestive faculties of the same combinations played by an orchestra. Their occasional harshness was softened by discreet distribution among instruments of appropriately diverse range and character, their richness intensified by saturation in rich orchestral sound.

When exploited by the great orchestral composers of the last half of the nineteenth century, these resources brought both composer and audience to a point where orchestration began to be confused with composition, where the distinction between art and artifice was lost in the intoxication of an unexampled variety and wealth of orchestral colour and the imposing splendour of orchestral sound.

The influence, on musical form, of preoccupation with harmonic effect, has been noted in a previous chapter, and particularly the tendency to substitute an amorphous structure of colour and mood for the classical elements of a vertical harmony and melodic-rhythmic lines and contours. Without the orchestra this development would have been impossible, at least to the same degree. For the combination of harmonic and orchestral resources gave to an amorphous structure a dynamic formal substance of sheer sound.

It is customary to speak of modern orchestration as having begun with Berlioz. This is true as far as pure orchestration is concerned. It was the *Symphonie Fantastique* that pointed the way to a type of composition built around harmonic and orchestral metamorphoses of a single theme in defiance of traditional concepts of form. But the trend, of which the orchestra proved to be the decisive instrument, may more properly be said to have begun with Beethoven. With him began the intensive exploitation of those dramatic faculties inherent in the diatonic scale that have contributed more than anything else to the popular assumption that music "means" something. With him the development of dynamics as a decisive element in musical structure approached maturity. The great provider of dynamic effects was the symphony orchestra.

Beethoven was not, certainly, the first composer to write dramatic music. There is drama in the operas of Gluck, Mozart and even Cherubini. But Beethoven was distinguished from the others in that almost all his music was dramatic. Whereas earlier composers could, when the situation required, write dramatically, Beethoven could hardly write otherwise. Pertinent in this connection is Paul Henry Lang's comment

"We still do not realize the tremendous impact of Beethoven's music on the succeeding generations. We know that instrumental music was under his spell for the rest of the century, but there is still no department of music that does not owe him his very soul. Beethoven endowed pure instrumental music with the most intense and expressive dramatic accents, an expressiveness that cast its reflection on dramatic music itself. A circle closes here; opera-born symphony now helps to create the language of the modern music-drama. The tremendous power and sharp edge of this music, its fervour and warmth, but, above all, its animated contrasts were eminently dramatic."[21]

Lang's observation that "opera-born symphony now helps to create the language of the modern music-drama" is especially perspicacious. He might have been even more pat. He could have said: "Opera-born symphony becomes symphony-born opera." From Beethoven's time onward all symphonic music was to become, in view of its prevailing dramatic and descriptive substance, more or less operatic, while opera, at the same time, was to become increasingly symphonic.

Throughout the first half of the nineteenth century the concept of opera as a form in which singers are the protagonists was to hold its own, despite the steady growth of the orchestra in size and importance in the works of Weber, Meyerbeer and Verdi. But after Wagner the scales were tipped irrevocably in favour of the symphonic concept. The orchestra became the protagonist, and responsibility for dramatic continuity and articulation shifted from the stage to the pit.

In its modest origins in the seventeenth-century Italian opera, the orchestra provided an opportunity for part-playing by instruments of different timbres and ranges. It gave singers a more plastic, more flexible, more mobile, more expressive, more varied, and less obtrusive accompaniment than was possible on instruments plucked or struck. It also provided an opportunity for varying a predominantly vocal entertainment with instrumental inter-ludes, an opportunity that was, in the course of time, to lead to orchestral independence—hence Lang's reference to the "opera-born symphony". To the basic string quintet the woodwinds added variety of colour and the contrasts that made multiple-voiced part writing easier to follow. The brass added brilliance and emphasis, and the percussion instruments contributed to the din when that was wanted—if not much, as we have seen, to the pulse.

Mozart and Haydn drew upon all these resources and achieved an instrumentation, not only beautifully balanced in sound, but also beautifully balanced in purpose. Theirs was an orchestra ideally designed to serve the expression of musical thought and invention, and ideally employed by the composers in that service. Just as they perfected the resources of tonal harmony, worked out and passed along to them by hundreds of seventeenth- and eighteenth-century Italian, German, French and English composers culminating in Bach, so also they perfected the essentially musical resources of the orchestra. They also completed the instrumental forms that had slowly evolved from the dance suites, sonatas, toccatas, sinfonias, concerti grossi and over-tures of their predecessors, and achieved the classical symphony which was to serve structurally as a model for emulation or as a point of departure for every composer who came after them.

Prior to their time and, indeed, in their own youth, orchestration had been a haphazard affair. Since most music was written for a particular place, often for specific occasion, orchestration was determined more by the availability of instruments and the reputed abilities of the available players than by any special sound-effects a composer may have had in mind, to be played by one certain combination of instruments and no other.

In any case, the choice of instruments beyond those of the basic string quintet was limited. Only oboes, bassoons, trumpets and horns were in more or less common use, and they doubled more often than they went their independent and characteristic way. Their mechanical imperfections so restricted their capacities in tone, intonation, tonality, range and velocity that there could be no question of their being employed as they and many additional instruments are employed today.

In these circumstances it is hardly surprising that scoring was so little a matter of concern that, like the writing out of inner parts within the general harmonic scheme, it was frequently left to copyists. Indeed, the completion of the composer's harmonic purpose was commonly left to the harpsichord-player (often the composer himself) who proceeded from the well-understood hieroglyphics of a figured-bass, much as the jazz pianist today proceeds from the chord-designations of a popular tune. That the harpsichord was the basic instrument of the primitive orchestra speaks for itself. As William Wallace, in his article on orchestration in *Grove's Dictionary*, remarked:

"Composers appear to have been occupied more with the construction of their theme than with the manner of presenting it. Lully was content to write the melody and the bass, leaving the middle parts, and such scoring as was requisite, to his copyists. . . . Gretry was equally indifferent, and it was said of his scores that you could drive a coach-and-four between the treble and the bass."[15]

After Haydn and Mozart there could be no more talk of

leaving the scoring and the filling in of middle voices to copyists and apprentices. For in these details, as well as in thematic invention and structure, lay the substance of future musical creation and individual stylistic distinction. After Beethoven came Berlioz and the whole history of evolutionary development that would make it possible, less than a hundred years later, for a Rimsky-Korsakov to say that "to orchestrate is to create", and prompt a Schönberg to attempt, in the third of his *Five Orchestral Pieces*, Opus 16, an experiment in which tone colour is the sole substance. Again to cite Wallace:

"While the orchestra was growing in strength, its development was to have a profound effect upon composition. The art was being rent within itself by discord. Five years after the first performance of Beethoven's *Choral Symphony* there came the *Symphonie Fantastique* of Berlioz. The one was incomprehensible to many, the other devastating. Whatever the views that were held, it is clear that a rift had appeared, and that tradition on its complacent side had received a shock. . . . Some felt that the frontier of music had been extended."

The significance of this is subsequently more precisely defined when in dealing with Berlioz, Wallace states: "It is not certain where composition with him ended and orchestration began."

In short, the "infallible test of the piano" was no longer applicable. Mozart's and Haydn's orchestral compositions all sound well when played on the piano, and give musical pleasure, for they are derived from purely musical elements of melody and rhythm, and the structure is fundamentally harmonic. The same may be said in lesser degree of Beethoven, Schubert, Schumann and Brahms. At least, their orchestral music has had extensive and profitable currency in two- and four-hand piano arrangements. It cannot be said of Berlioz, Liszt, Wagner, Strauss, Bruckner and Mahler.

Herein, I think, lies the explanation of the curious circumstance that those critics in the nineteenth century who espoused Mendelssohn, Schumann and Brahms were considered reactionary, even though the composers themselves were contemporary and far from mere imitators of their hallowed predecessors. Both Schumann and Brahms made their respective contributions to the extension of harmonic freedom. Their music may correctly be regarded, in the conventional sense, as representing an advance over the music of, say, Beethoven and Schubert. They were even dramatic in the sense of the word as it applies to the instrumental music of Beethoven.

The question was rather one of definition. As Wallace says, "A rift had appeared." Brahms and Schumann, for all the romantic-dramatic elements in their music, remained true to the classical concepts of musical form based on melodic, harmonic and rhythmic structure, and never achieved great distinction as orchestrators. The others tended towards a concept of form deriving from elements rather philosophical, psychological, literary, poetic, or graphic than musical—in other words programme music, or the tone poem, for which orchestration was a primary technique. After Brahms the line between symphony and symphonic poem became blurred, no matter how careful such subsequent composers of symphonies as Tchaikovsky, Dvořák, Franck, Bruckner, Mahler and Sibelius may have been to designate their symphonies as such and to underline the designation by adherence to the conventional three- or four-movement structural plan.

Not that there was no music in tone poetry. It continued to exploit musical elements of melody, harmony and rhythm, but the expression could no longer be regarded as purely musical. Or, to put it more precisely, what was thus musically expressed was intended and assumed to be something more than merely music. Tone poetry was inspired by a literary model, by a poem, a picture, a vision, a philosophical concept or a psychological problem, and was supposed to project a musical approximation or representation, a paraphrase, as it were, of the literary or graphic original.

The basic, indispensable instrument of tone poetry was the orchestra, although not, to be sure, the orchestra of Haydn and Mozart. Schumann and Brahms would live on through their vocal, solo instrument, and chamber music if all the symphony orchestras in the world were abolished tomorrow. But what would be left of the others—of Berlioz, Liszt, Wagner, Strauss, Bruckner, Mahler and even Schönberg and Berg?

Not much of any consequence! To say that they orchestrated rather than composed is a tempting but inadmissible generalization, although it is certainly true of many of their inferiors. But it is hardly too much to say that their works were conceived orchestrally. Removed from the orchestra, they are ineffective on their purely musical substance alone.

Whereas Mozart, Haydn, Beethoven, Schubert, Mendelssohn, Schumann and Brahms used the orchestra as a means of enrichment, the others used it rather as a means of articulation. Where the classicists thought in terms of musical effects orchestrally executed, the others began to think of instrumental effects more or less musically ordered. Whatever was done was considered justified as long as the "effect" was enhanced or heightened. Sound rather than

purely musical organization became the sustaining substance of composition, and orchestration became a basic
structural element. This accounts for the present conventional disparagement of transcription and its sanctimonious
extension to the obviously transcription-proof music of
older composers who made a habit of transcribing for any
handy combination anything they thought worth the effort.

For the student of contemporary music the significant
factor is that in the long-drawn-out battle between the
classicists and the romanticists, or between the musicians
and the tone poets, the latter carried the day and determined
the course of musical evolution up to the time of the First
World War.

As a consequence, the contemporary composer inherited
an instrument hardly capable either of further growth or of
further refinement. There was no transcending the transcendentalism of Mahler's *Symphony of a Thousand*. One
could not improve upon the graphic and prosaic description
of Strauss' *Sinfonia Domestica*. It was difficult to imagine
more lustrous canvases than Debussy's *La Mer* and *Iberia*.
Romantic, philosophic pretentiousness seemed to have
reached a limit with Schönberg's *Gurrelieder*. Just as
Stravinsky's *Le Sacré du Printemps* marked the ultimate in
brutal primitive stylization, so Ravel's *Daphnis and Chloe*
carried orgiastic pagan riotousness to its limit. *Salome* and
*Elektra* had touched the extremes of sexual pathology, and
orchestration could hardly be richer than that of *Der
Rosenkavalier*.

In other words, the contemporary composer inherited an
instrument not only rather more than perfect, but also
tailored to the specifications of a particular approach to
composition. For less grandiose purposes it was overgrown

and unwieldy, uneconomical both musically and financially. Faced with the inadvisability of trying to outdo his immediate predecessors in the kind of music which had produced this sensitive monster, the contemporary composer found himself with a lot more orchestra on his hands than he could profitably use.

In this respect it is certainly not insignificant that the inevitable reaction was led, not by wild-eyed reformers, but by such sober men as Strauss, Schönberg, Bartók, Stravinsky and Ravel. They had all participated in the orchestra's "Götterdämmerung" in the first decade of the century and learned from their own experience that enough was enough—that the outer limits of music's capacities in the dramatic and descriptive directions pointed by Beethoven and Berlioz had been reached. Obviously this was not purely an orchestral phenomenon. It was part and parcel of a general exhaustion involving the whole problem of harmonic substance and structure. But the orchestra had provided the last rich technical resource, and had made possible a few glorious years of grace following Wagner's raid on the capital resources of chromatic harmony. Now even the orchestra was incapable of further expansion and refinement, and the composers had no choice but to turn back.

A. Schönberg, whose *Gurrelieder* had required twenty-five woodwind instruments and twenty-five brass, turned to a chamber orchestra of as few as fifteen players. Stravinsky, whose *Le Sacré* had employed eighteen each of woodwinds and brass, reacted similarly. Even Strauss, whose *Sinfonia Domestica*, had called for a piccolo, three flutes, two oboes, oboe d'amore, English horn, clarinet in D, clarinet in A, two clarinets in B flat, bass clarinet, four saxophones, four bassoons, double bassoon, eight horns, four trumpets, three trombones, bass tuba, four timpani, triangle, tambourine, glockenspiel, cymbals, bass drum and two harps, turned after *Der Rosenkavalier*, to more modest ensembles and achieved in *Ariadne auf Naxos*, something that critics to this day see fit to call Mozartian. The others followed suit.

It is difficult even now to determine how far this reaction was prompted by a sincere revulsion against turn-of-the-century transcendentalism—by a recognition of the fact that a bigger orchestra does not necessarily make better or even more important music—and how far it was simply an unspoken admission that further expansion could lead only to disintegration and that retreat was the only sensible alternative. Doubtless it was a little of both. What the composers have written in their numerous books and articles betrays a desire to return to a more musical music, or at least to a less pretentious, a less cumbersome and a less expensive apparatus. But there is also rather more than a mere suggestion that there was not much else that they could do.

The composer's primary concern has been with the impossibility of further harmonic expansion within the framework of the tonal system. Since the expansion of harmony and the expansion of the orchestra had been so closely integrated and so interdependent, the composer seems to have assumed that the impasse was inevitably common to both. In a sense, of course, he was right; for what is done with instruments is determined by style and the composer's objectives within the style, and for the past fifty years the serious composer has had no style. Burdened with the need for harmonic originality, and unable any longer to achieve it without destroying the harmonic system, he could not be original in the orchestra, either. His lack of progress in the orchestra is simply a reflection of his lack of progress anywhere else. Foundering with his other materials, he has foundered with the orchestra, too.

There was still plenty of opportunity for orchestral originality, however, and it was exploited, not by the serious composer, but by the jazz arranger who, having a different frame of technical and expressive reference, and unburdened by the necessity for harmonic originality, could evolve a new style and orchestrate freely according to objectives appropriate to that style. That he ultimately evolved an entirely new orchestra should not deceive us as to its European origin. What the arranger owes to Strauss, Debussy, Ravel and even the early Stravinsky must be obvious to anyone who has listened to any of the varieties of big band from Guy Lombardo through Goodman and Ellington to Herman and Basie.

Unlike the serious composer, the arranger knew what he wanted, and could shape his orchestra accordingly, just as the European composers of the nineteenth century, starting with the modest orchestra of Haydn and Mozart, shaped it to meet their new requirements. The arranger restored the piano to a position roughly equivalent to that occupied by the harpsichord or piano in the baroque orchestra. He discarded the strings but kept the double bass, which, now free of the cumbersome bow, assists the piano in providing harmonic and rhythmic guidance and support, just as it did in the baroque orchestra. He added the saxophones and greatly increased the responsibilities of the brass. The gifted trumpet and trombone players showed how much more could be done than serious composers had ever dreamed of. Above all there was the evolution of the drums as the pulsating heart of the ensemble in a manner for which there is no parallel in the European orchestra, if only because the explicit beat has never been a basic element in European music.

Serious composers—some of them, at least—have observed the evolution of the jazz orchestra with admiration and envy, even if with some distaste for the music that produced it. If it did not appear to them as evidence of their own failure, this was because they could always say, and quite justly, that it was associated with musical purposes foreign to their own. There is little consolation in this. Committed to their own purposes and to traditional means of accomplishing them, they have made no comparable progress, and it is unlikely that they ever will.

# THE EXECUTIVE MUSICIAN

IF, IN OUR VIEW of the crisis of evolution in serious music, we have concentrated thus far on the problems of the composer, this has been because the root crisis is the composer's inability to proceed any further with his inherited materials in a manner appropriate to his traditional objectives as a serious composer and at the same time agreeable and stimulating to his lay listeners.

But the composer is not alone in his despair, nor alone in experiencing the consequences of his perplexity. His inability to provide viable new music has imposed upon the executive musician the unwelcome role of an antiquarian specializing in music fifty to three hundred and fifty years old. The executive musician's problems are less spectacularly obvious, since he can still make do with the inherited materials, and is expected to do so. But he is denied the stimulation of expanding the horizons of his musical experience by introducing to his listeners any contemporary music reasonably likely to earn their approval, and he is also denied the stimulation of expanding the capacities of his instrument. He is, in short, compelled to live as a musician without a music of his own.

To compare him, for a moment, with the jazz musician may help to reveal the desperate nature of his plight, for during precisely the period whem the stagnation of serious music has been growing apparent, the jazz musician, working in a different idiom and with music, not only of his own time but also largely of his own making, has radically extended the traditional technical and expressive horizons of such older instruments as the piano, trumpet, clarinet, double bass and guitar; and established previously unimagined standards for new instruments such as the saxophones and vibraphone—not to mention the sheerly phenomenal contribution of the jazz percussion player.

Like the European musician of the eighteenth and nineteenth centuries, he builds a new repertoire to accommodate his technical advance as an instrumentalist and at the same time to satisfy his listeners' taste for novelty. The serious musician, by contrast, is stuck with a repertoire tailored to the technical capacities and interpretive predilections of musicians of a hundred or a hundred and fifty years ago. Nor is that all. He is further restricted to those few masterpieces that have survived the test of time and do not sound impossibly old-fashioned.

Take, for example, the concerto literature. For really sure-fire items today the violinist is pretty much restricted to the Beethoven and Brahms concertos. There are a number of Mozart concertos available to him, although they will not draw as well, and the Mendelssohn Concerto is optional. Prokofiev, Sibelius, Khatchaturian, Bartók, Schönberg and Berg can be drawn upon as novelties, but there is no great audience for them. And how much of an audience is there today even for the concertos of Tchaikovsky, Bruch, Glazounov and Spohr?

Fifty years ago there was an audience not only for these but also for the concertos of Wieniawski, Vieuxtemps, Paganini, de Beriot, Viotti, Hubay, Sarasate and Joachim. Some of their music is still taught in the colleges, but concert-wise it has gone by the board. Today's concert violinist, unless, like Menuhin, he chooses to appear as

champion of the unfamiliar, is fated to go through life
playing the Beethoven and Brahms concertos week after
week, night after night, to the end of his days.

It is the same for the pianist. He has the Mozart,
Beethoven, Brahms and Schumann concertos, and that's
about all. The Chopin concertos are inferior to Chopin's
recital pieces. The Liszt concertos are already beginning to
sound too tacky to use before a sophisticated public, and
they lack the melodic sweep that guarantees the Rachmaninoff, Grieg and Tchaikovsky concertos some further
viability, if almost in a semi-classical category. The Mendelssohn, Saint-Saëns and MacDowell concertos are dated,
not to mention those of Moszkovsky and Anton Rubinstein.
Nor are the Bartók and Prokofiev concertos likely to ease
the burden on the standard works.

Symphonically it is not much different. The Haydn
symphonies are not box-office, and of the Mozart symphonies only the last three and possibly the *Haffner* may be
counted on to draw. With Beethoven the odd-numbered run
well ahead of the other four. Schubert's symphonies in
B minor and C major are still viable, and so are all four by
Brahms and the last three by Tchaikovsky, César Franck
and Dvořák are fading. Mahler and Bruckner draw nowhere but in central Europe, and, very recently, in London;
Sibelius draws only in the United States and England—
presumably also in Finland, Mendelssohn's symphonies are
peripheral. Schumann's are of little account, popularly
speaking. That Saint-Saëns, Spohr, Bizet, Balakirev and a
score or more of less prominent German and French composers ever wrote symphonies has long been as good as
forgotten. Apart from the symphonies, the truly attractive
orchestral repertoire is generally restricted to three of

Strauss' tone poems, the Wagner excerpts and a few odd pieces by Debussy, Ravel and Stravinsky. Even Liszt's *Les Preludes* is beginning to sound old hat, not to speak of *Scheherazade*, *Bolero*, the *Slavonic Rhapsodies* and De Falla's *España*.

The above is obviously an indulgence in generalities. Any number of borderline cases may be cited, and I may well have omitted some works and some composers that really draw. The problem is further complicated by the difficulty of determining with reasonable accuracy just which piece or pieces on a programme of four or five is the one that attracts the paying public. It is also complicated by the difficulty of gauging box-office reactions to individual pieces or programmes where subscriptions account for anything between seventy-five and ninety per cent of the audience. There is, of course, the test of the non-subscription concert or request programme, and here, I believe, the composition of such programmes the world over will support the correctness of the selections that I have just made. It will, at least, indicate that the promoters of such programmes agree with me.

And then there is an infinity of marginal or regional differences. One may cite the fact that such symphonists as Shostakovitch, Sibelius and Prokofiev have an audience of sorts in England and the United States but are practically unknown in Central Europe, where the equivalent place is occupied by Bruckner, Mahler and Pfitzner. Nevertheless, the listing above is probably essentially correct, if not entirely complete. And it justifies the question: how long can this repertoire survive the present frequency and multiplicity of its repetition, and what parts of it will survive longest?

One may assume that it will never vanish from the face of the earth. Works that have survived so many generations have automatically demonstrated their superiority over music that is valid for merely a score of years or so. Their places are assured among the historic masterpieces of artistic production. They will always be of interest and afford pleasure to people whose curiosity and enthusiasm transcend the fashions of their own time, however good or bad the latter may be. At the present time they are clearly doing more than that, although it is equally clear that the repertoire is steadily diminishing. Possibly more compositions are played, but it is the drawing power of ever fewer that makes their performance possible.

Until about forty years ago the problem of repertoire was subdued, as it is in jazz today, by the constant addition of new viable music or new ways of playing older music. The pieces that orchestras and virtuosos played were largely contemporary. Virtuosos such as Bach, Mozart, Beethoven, Spohr, Thalberg, Moscheles, Kalkbrenner, Field, Paganini, Vieuxtemps, Wieniawski, Bull, Chopin, Liszt and—in our own time—Kreisler and Rachmaninoff, all tended to favour their own compositions. They were extending the technical horizons of their instruments, as the jazz musician does today, and what they had inherited from the repertoire of their predecessors was insufficiently challenging. They had also to adjust to the changing tastes of their listeners.

In any case, the listener felt himself part of a continuing evolution, aware not only of a great tradition but also of a lively and promising contemporary production. The oldest music he heard at the turn of the century was, moreover, sixty years younger than it is today. This makes a difference. So do the facts that there were fewer performances, fewer performers, fewer performing institutions and no recording.

Until very recently the increasing stagnation of the repertoire was obscured by the constantly improving standard of performance. The repertoire ceased to grow substantially, and the vision, as far as the audience was concerned, was backward rather than forward. The feeling of being part of a continuing evolution, which had so fascinated the listener at the end of the nineteenth century was frustrated by every new composition. But one could rejoice in the presence of conductors and other executants who made the old works live as they had never lived before. Or seemed to.

Then came recording. The introduction of the symphony orchestra, the virtuoso and the opera house into home and school, particularly after the advent of the long-playing record, undoubtedly increased the interested audience; so did the growth of musical appreciation classes and the emergence of a sizeable literature on the appreciation and enjoyment of classical music. Hundreds of thousands of compliant people were easily persuaded that a modest familiarity with and a reasonable taste for European music was indispensable to one who would be thought cultured in a culture-conscious society. It would be risky to say that records and education have passed the peak of their influence as audience recruiters, but the contribution made by improved performances is probably a thing of the past, if only because further improvement seems unlikely. All that is left is improvement of reproduction. But the question is not really whether musicians may yet emerge from the younger generation capable of playing even more brilliantly than their famous predecessors. This is altogether possible, even likely. It is a question rather of how much more brilliance the standard repertoire can take, a question of whether the standard pieces offer opportunities for the full exploitation of the gifts and accomplishments of the new musician.

Prior to the First World War the evolution of European music in terms of composition went hand in hand with the growing capacity of the musician and the increasing efficiency and scope of the instruments he used. The composer tended to demand more than either musicians or their instruments had previously been expected to yield. The mechanical advances in the construction of pianos and wind instruments offered both composers and virtuosos—often, as we have seen, combined in the same person—new possibilities.

The evolution of piano music, for instance, was inseparable from the physical evolution of the piano and the exploitation of its growing potentialities by composers and pianists and composer-pianists from Beethoven to Rachmaninoff. Nothing essential has been added to the piano or the technical requirements of the master executant for fifty years, excepting possibly the percussive uses made of it by such comparatively recent composers as Bartók and Prokofiev. What this means may be illuminated if we remember that neither Mozart nor Beethoven, without extensive preparation and musical reorientation, could, in all likelihood, have played a Liszt concerto or one of his or Chopin's tougher études, while Liszt could, very probably, have played with relative ease anything that has been written since his time.

What has changed since Liszt's time is the number of pianists who can meet the standards he set. What was unique with Liszt and Chopin is today's prerequisite for professional status, with the inevitable consequence that it becomes harder and harder for one pianist to stand out strikingly above others. It is not that there may not be some truly exceptional or unique talents. Indeed, there certainly are. But it is no longer possible, by pianistic accomplishment alone, to stand out so conspicuously from one's rivals. The mean standard has risen astronomically, but the pieces to which these standards are applied remain the same. Even a Van Cliburn is inhibited by technical requirements already several generations old. The exceptional talent of today must write his own music. There is nothing written to show what he really can or cannot do, at least in the serious field.

But as a composer the virtuoso is inhibited by the same problems of exhausted resources as those which frustrate any other composer as long as he is restricted to the technical and expressive frame of reference of serious music. And he cannot escape this frame of reference without compromising his status as a serious musician. He can, like Friedrich Gulda, find new and contemporary outlets and challenges in jazz, but if he does so, he is looked upon askance by the serious musical community where his heaviest investments of time, training and even money have been made, and is likely to be regarded as something of an intruder in the odd world of jazz.

Thus he has, in the end, no choice but to attempt to outdo his colleagues in the old music. This is producing some singular results, including a good deal of spirited and agitated riding of dispirited old war horses. We hear the old pieces played faster, louder, more easily, more casually, more excitedly, more flawlessly, more recklessly and more preciously than they have ever been played before. It is no longer a question of the pianist surviving the repertoire. It

D

is rather a question of the repertoire surviving the pianist. It cannot yield, without cost to its structure and content, the distortion exacted by the new virtuoso pianist in his search for a challenge and for the marginal differentiation required to set himself off perceptibly from his fellows.

What has been said here of the pianist by way of illustration is true of other instruments, including the instruments of the orchestra—in so far as they are restricted to the European idiom—and of the orchestra itself as a collective instrument. The violin literature has been complete, as far as its technical requirements are concerned, for many generations, and it is unlikely that anyone will ever play it better than the best violinists of the present time. The balance of technical sovereignty and interpretive mastery in the playing of a Heifetz or an Oistrakh is pretty fine, and probably close to the maximum in both aspects.

Orchestras have reached a point of perfection, particularly in the United States, which is already exposing them to complaints of machine-like precision, an indication of distortion on the side of technical brilliance beyond what is required for the ultimately satisfactory projection of a given piece of music. It is simply a fact that nowadays, the wind instruments and their players being as good as they are, first-class orchestral musicians accomplish with ease the most difficult tasks any composer has ever given them. Indeed, the instruments can do a lot more, as can be heard any day in any one of a score of first-rate jazz bands. But the orchestral player, like the virtuoso, is inhibited by a repertoire which came into being under entirely different technical and expressive circumstances.

All this being the case, what remains to hold the audience's attention, to excite astonishment and admiration, to give that element of suspense and surprise which is an integral, if possibly not the noblest part of any audience's participation in a concert? Along with an audience's enjoyment of beautiful music the spectacle of the uniquely gifted or accomplished individual producing something beyond the norm of human experience exercises a fundamentally attractive force. And this is rare these days. Plenty of young professionals and even students can play anything that Liszt or Paganini alone could play a hundred years ago, and the letter-perfect orchestral performance of the most difficult pieces is now the rule rather than the exception.

Until recently the answer has seemed to lie with the conductor. A score or so of instrumental virtuosos can still make a tolerably exciting evening, but even the virtuoso prospers best these days as soloist with the orchestra, where alone he may be reasonably extended technically and interpretively in compositions of appropriate dimensions and under circumstances where lay audiences are favourably disposed to such undertakings by the imposing presence of a symphony orchestra.

Our century has seen the conductor achieve supremacy. He has come a long way from the Kapellmeister seated at the harpsichord, or concert-master gesticulating with his bow, to the all-powerful dictator of a hundred odd men, imposing his assumed conceptual genius and insight upon the intelligence of lesser musicians and bending them to his interpretive will. He is the supreme choreographer elaborating a memorized score. But even the conductor is now facing the operation of the law of diminishing returns. He could continue to grow as an executive institution as long as he could teach, persuade, cajole, inveigle, browbeat and drive an orchestra to play better than other orchestras had played under previous conductors, and as long as he as an individual could plumb deeper in the yet unexplored depths of the symphonic masterpieces.

It is largely to the conductor that we owe the present ultimately high standard of orchestral performance. It was he—in the persons of Spohr, Wagner, Liszt, Herbeck, Levi, Buelow, Richter, Mottl, Nikisch, Mahler and Weingartner, on up to the great conductors of our own experience—who had the visions of what could yet be done, and demonstrated how much more could be obtained from men and from their instruments. As a virtuoso the conductor matured later than the pianist or the violinist. It has been the privilege of our time to experience his maturation.

His achievements have not been without cost, however, in terms of the balance between composer and interpreter, any more than they have been without cost in the case of the violinist and the pianist. They have obviously drawn excessive attention to the conductor's person, and for a good many years now the central point of interest in most orchestral programmes has been, not the familiar composition, but what the conductor has been able to do with it. He has usurped the dominant position in musical life formerly held by singers, pianists and violinists.

Even this situation had its virtues as long as fertile areas of interpretive and technical soil remained unexplored and unexploited within the standard symphonic repertoire. It seems unlikely now that any such areas remain—which is not to say that interpretive evolution in respect to the symphonic repertoire has run its course. The tastes of an audience and fashions in interpretation are subject to continuous change, if only because people change from year to year and from generation to generation. But the changes that one has observed in the past decade do not suggest that the new generation of conductors, any more than the new generation of piano and violin virtuosos, is headed towards new revelations of the spiritual depths of the masterpieces; or that the orchestral performance, any more than that on the violin or piano, can advance constructively beyond the peak of near-perfection it has now attained.

What one hears now, particularly from the younger conductors—as is also true of the younger virtuosos—smacks more of efficiency, eccentricity, idiosyncrasy and desperate seeking after new effects. Assuming that some element of distortion is inherent in any artistic product; assuming that distortion is, indeed, an element of the artistic and interpretive concept; and assuming that such conductors as Toscanini and Furtwängler achieved just that extent of distortion required to set the great masterpieces off in the most strikingly proportioned outline, then we frequently find in the kind of performance becoming fashionable today a situation where the point of maximum tolerable distortion has been transgressed. The symptoms are excessively fast tempi, excessive and capricious tempo changes and rubati, and excessive dynamic contrasts. The long line is sacrificed for undue attention to the maximum exploitation of the individual phrase. Inner parts and secondary episodes are drawn out of context. Repose is sacrificed to restless agitation, suggesting conductors unsure both of themselves and their audiences.

The assumption of a "maximum possible distortion" may be an over-simplification as far as the audience is concerned, which is why one may refer to this type of interpretation as fashionable. Conductors and instrumental

virtuosos who indulge in such excesses enjoy the applause
of both professional critics and lay audiences. This is understandable. Repetition of familiar masterpieces requires that
they be differently and ever more excitingly performed.
With contemporary composers failing to provide excitement
with new compositions, the old works must be made to
yield it. The conductor and the virtuoso replace the default-
ing composer as an instrument for keeping the repertoire
up to date. This was all right as long as there was still room,
or margin, for legitimate improvement. But the question
remains: how far can the symphonic masterpieces be
stretched to bridge the gap in listening habits between the
generation of their origin and our own generation and
the generations to come?

Two things seem certain: (1) the gap grows wider and
wider with each successive generation, and (2) there is a
limit to the elasticity of the standard masterpiece, even to a
Beethoven Ninth Symphony. The younger conductors and
virtuosos attempt to bridge the gap with a compromise
between the requirements of the modern audience and the
scripture of fading masterpieces. Thus far they have not
discovered the outer limits of the masterpieces' elasticity,
which are, to be sure, an indeterminate factor, established
by the amount of distortion audiences can accommodate
without losing their sense of identity with the familiar
compositions.

There is more to the problem, however, than simply
the passing of the peak of technical perfection within the
technical framework of the familiar composition or the
passing of the point of ideal distortion in the interpretive
representation of masterpieces, as insoluble as each of these
may be. The achievement of ideal distortion is possible only

to a man endowed with an ideal identification with the composer and his style. Without this he cannot have that sure sense of the limits of the outer boundaries of interpretive space, the instinct that tells him "just so far and no farther", the feeling for what is permissible in any given episode in relation to the whole. This is usually summarized as a "sense of form", but the term has little meaning if divorced from the corollary "sense of content" and "sense of style".

This was borne in upon some of us by the death of Furtwängler, upon many others, no doubt, by the deaths of Koussevitzky and Rachmaninoff, Toscanini and Josef Hofmann. What was lost in each case was not just a great musician, but a living bridge to the age when the compositions which they conducted and played best had originated, or at least to an age closer to the originals than our own. They had a personal identification with, and a personal devotion to the compositions they played best which younger men, no matter how gifted, cannot possibly have.

It used to be said of Furtwängler and Rachmaninoff, particularly by younger musicians under the influence of Toscanini's much praised and to some extent mythical or misunderstood exactitude, that they took liberties with the music. They certainly did. But they were liberties guaranteed by an unerring instinct for the appropriate, based in turn upon an identification with the composer, and fortified by a kind of faith and affinity for which intelligence is no substitute. What they achieved was more richly communicative, more memorably moving than the academic immaculateness achieved today by certain of our less adventurous younger musicians who flatter themselves that by playing the notes exactly as written they arrive at a more honest and respectable result. Certainly their liberties were

preferable to the distortions indulged by the contemporary
seekers after effect two or three generations farther removed
from the source.

It is simply a fact that the younger musician of today
cannot feel about Beethoven and Brahms and Wagner the
way Furtwängler did, however, good a musician he may be,
and however honest his affection and admiration for the
music. The change in environment is too great. The same is
true of the audience. Furtwängler could carry a contemporary audience back fifty or a hundred years in time because
his knowledge of the way inspired the audience's confidence
and because his zeal enlisted its enthusiastic co-operation.
The younger musician cannot do it. He may, as a good
contemporary musician, play Beethoven to the satisfaction
of a contemporary audience, but both musician and audience
continue at their own risk, neither of them being too sure
either of the point of departure or the destination.

Nor can a slavish imitation of the Furtwängler records
—or the records of Rachmaninoff, Hofmann, Toscanini,
Kreisler, Paderewski, etc.—solve the problem. Without the
inner identification and without the faith and conviction
proceeding from it, such an imitation would be a dead thing,
no matter how exact the reproduction. One can duplicate
the tempi and the accents, but there is no duplicating the
fire that sustained them.

One may argue that the loss is less radical than I have
pictured it, that tradition is handed down from generation
to generation, and that the loss of a bridge to the past in the
death of a Furtwängler or a Rachmaninoff may be dis-
counted by the number of younger musicians and listeners
who may be assumed to have been guided across it by them.
Something is passed on, to be sure, but not all. There is

dilution at every step along the way, rendered inevitable by the number of new environmental factors influencing the lives, habits and ways of thinking of each new generation of musicians and listeners. Traditions could be handed down for hundreds of years in unchanging peasant societies. But they cannot survive unblemished the social changes to which modern society is exposed from generation to generation.

Under these new circumstances the feeling of identification cannot be passed on, or at least it cannot be passed on completely. Man is inescapably of his time, or something close to his time. Furtwängler, whose devotion to the romantics was such that he could never achieve a proper identification with music later than that of the young Richard Strauss, was practically a case of arrested development, musically speaking; which was why his identification was more intense than that of his contemporaries. He was a phenomenon through whom audiences of this generation were privileged to get closer to Beethoven than would normally have been possible for people living a hundred years and more after a composer's death. The more usual phenomenon is what we find among so many of the younger conductors and virtuosos of today who are obviously more at ease in Strauss, Debussy, Ravel, Shostakovitch, Prokofiev and Bartók than in the classics or the romantics. Most of this music is not, to be sure, exactly of our time, but it is a lot closer to it.

Assuming, then, that the new styles of interpreting the standards will find both performer and listener drifting farther and farther away from the conceptual and technical origin, seeking new sources of excitement and new areas of distinctive marginal difference between one performance and another, then it must be simply a matter of time until excessive distortion, or excessive academicism, not now recognized as such, becomes unmistakable caricature. At that point—and it will be reached sooner, of course, with some pieces than with others—the limit of elasticity will have been found, and it will be all up with the symphony orchestra, the virtuoso conductor and the virtuoso instrumentalist—and what we know as the symphonic repertoire.

# THE CRITIC

HARDLY MORE ENVIABLE than the position of the composer, faced with an indifferent audience and exhausted materials, or that of the performer, condemned to go on playing the same music year in and year out, is that of the critic, who must hear more of the uninviting new music and more of the well-worn masterpieces than other people do and manage somehow to put a good face upon it.

He has little choice in the matter. Our musical society has determined his proper role in life to be as much promoter and propagandist as critic. Such is the force of superstition and custom that today's critic accepts his inglorious status without complaint. It is not difficult to understand why.

Musical history or, more accurately, the folklore of musical appreciation, has made of the critic a figure of ignominy. The prototype is Wagner's Sixtus Beckmesser, the Meistersinger pedant who harps on the rules and defends an old system with which he is familiar against a new system with which he is not. He is the Philistine pitted against the forces of progress and enlightenment.

Ernest Newman summed up the situation tidily in the introduction to his edition of Chorley's *Thirty Years' Musical Recollections*:

"It is difficult," he wrote, "for the musical critic to achieve any immortality except one of opprobrium. He is remembered solely by his few misses; his many hits are not counted to him. The reason is obvious. If he talks sense, his views become the commonplaces of musical opinion, and no one thinks of crediting him in particular with them. If he talks nonsense, this is regarded as peculiarly his own, and is sure to be brought up against him by some musical biographer or other who wants to intensify the sympathetic atmosphere surrounding his hero by showing how sadly sympathy was lacking to him while he was alive."[16]

One has to look no farther than Mr. Newman himself to see how this works. In the introduction to his edition of Berlioz's *Memoirs* he wrote: "Thousands of people who have not the least idea how much good sense Chorley and Hanslick talked about music remember them for one or two mistakes they made about Wagner."[17] As Wagner's biographer this same Mr. Newman referred to Hanslick as a simpleton, and once went so far as to denounce him as "the most colossal ignoramus and charlatan who ever succeeded in imposing himself on an editor as a musical critic".[18]

This illustrates the problem nicely. As Wagner's biographer, Mr. Newman was writing a success story. Success was won against opposition, and is recognized as having been good for society. Therefore opposition was bad, and those who practised it were villains or fools.

As a critic, speaking for Chorley and Berlioz, Mr. Newman knew that it was not so simple. He knew that the critics about whom he wrote were well-informed and honest men who happened to hold opinions contrary to the consensus of society. Since society thinks that society is right, it must also assume that the critics were wrong.

Thus Mr. Newman's perspective changed as he moved from his position as critic to his position as biographer. In the latter role he committed precisely the sin of distortion which, as a critic, he accused other biographers of committing. It seems to have been a matter of whose bull was being gored. Historically speaking, society's bull has been the composer, and society has taken sides accordingly when composer and critic were in conflict.

To disparage this may seem to be claiming for the critic a position of special privilege. If the composer is required to accept collective judgment, then why not the critic? To which one might reply: precisely because he is a critic. The composer's job is to please his audience; the critic's to evaluate the pleasure. In this sense he is a critic, not only of composers and performers, but also of audiences. If he dissents from a favourable collective verdict he is, by implication, casting aspersions upon the tastes and discernment of the audiences that have reached the verdict. He therefore gets into trouble.

While it is plain, from this point of view, that the critic should not be answerable to collective judgment, since he would thus be forced into dull conformity, the historical record makes it equally plain that he is, in fact so answerable. He is judged, not by the quality of his criticism, but by whether or not his judgments have conformed to majority opinions. The unexciting respectability of contemporary criticism suggests that the historical lesson has not been lost on him. He has, of course, produced an appropriate rationalization, articulately expounded by Willi Schuh, one of the most reputable of European critics, in an essay in the 175th Anniversary Issue of the *Neue Züricher Zeitung*. Mr. Schuh writes:

"The 'great' epoch of music criticism lies far behind us. It is mourned neither by musicians nor the public. Least of all has the music critic himself any reason to desire a return to the partisan criticism of the nineteenth century. Only he who loves power for its own sake will regret that he is no

longer able to make or break composers and performers by
his personal verdict.

"In place of the 'bosses' (as Gustav Mahler used to call
them) and the real and would-be popes, we have today the
music expert, the commentator and interpreter who,
according to his knowledge, his musical sensibility, and his
ability to express himself in literate prose, creates for himself reputation and authority, but whose influence remains
limited. The advantage of the present situation lies in the
fact that artist and critic, despite the difference of their
positions, and despite unavoidable tensions, are no longer
identified with two separate, fundamentally hostile camps."

The foregoing is probably fairly representative of the
present appreciation of the critic's role and the objectives
of criticism. Especially characteristic is the derogatory
reference to the "partisan" criticism of the "great" epoch,
and the rather more than implied approval of a state of
affairs where the critic's new and socially approved function
is that of commentary and interpretation.

Mr. Schuh does, to be sure, subsequently qualify this
view. "If the trend of the time," he says, "is to put the
critic in a role of the artist's advocate and his intermediary
with the public, this is because criticism is confused with
musicology. The critic who is satisfied with explanation and
commentary is only half a critic. . . . He who has guided
his critical ship between the Scylla of poetic description
and the Charybdis of structural analysis now meets the real
task: to take a position on what he and his audience have
heard and to arrive at critical conclusions.

"Many critics today evade this responsibility. The
stubborn opponents of everything new have given way to a
new type of yes-man, who disguises with his claim to being

unopinionated the fact that he has no opinion at all. Many keep their better judgment to themselves in order to avoid being ridiculed by posterity, and confine themselves to non-committal descriptive explanation and analysis."

An admirably truthful statement! But how does it fit in with the previous abjuration of "partisan" critics of the past, and the approving recognition of a new order in which critics and artists are no longer split into "fundamentally hostile camps"? There would appear to be some ambivalence here. The critic wants to be a true critic, but he also wants an approved status as a constructive member of the artistic community. He may not be partisan, but still he may not dodge his obligation as a critic to arrive at conclusions and make evaluations. How is he to accomplish this?

It all depends on whether or not one accepts what Hindemith has called "the evolutionist's theory of music's increasing development towards higher goals".[9] Hindemith himself, like most composers, finds this theory untenable. But musical society accepts it without qualification—and has no choice but to condemn the hostile critic as an obstructionist.

The fact that the critic is as much, and usually as unwillingly, a victim of superstition as the lay listener, may explain why music criticism of this century has lacked a sense of adventure and become so dull. The calcification of the repertoire in the first decade of the century seems to have coincided with a calcification of society's thinking about music and musical history. It could not have happened at a worse time.

Wagner had conquered. Strauss had followed up his tone poems with *Salome*, *Elektra*, and *Der Rosenkavalier*. Stravinsky's ballets were the rage. Debussy had triumphed with *Pelléas et Mélisande*, Ravel with *Daphnis and Chloe*, Charpentier with *Louise*, and Puccini with *Madame Butterfly*. It looked like anything but a dead end. The Philistines were in flight. The present was glorious and the future bright. Critical romance was in flower.

Now, forty years later, the flower appears to have been made of imperishable wax. There has been no original thinking about music since then; at least, no original thinking has excited sufficient interest or proven sufficiently influential to shake society's faith in the conventions of critical thought as they existed in 1910.

Among these conventions the evolutionist's theory of progress was outstanding. The masterpieces of the nineteenth century had prevailed in the face of militant opposition. The "verdict of posterity" had fallen. It was: "All glory to the masterpieces and all ignominy to those who had opposed them!" The historical implications seemed to be that progress is inevitable and good, that opposition is ill-fated and bad.

So definitive was the verdict and so universal its acceptance forty years ago that henceforth few critics have dared or have even been disposed to challenge it. Ever since then, criticism has observed certain undocumented but well-understood bounds, among which the sanctity of the masterpieces and the assumption of infinite progress are the most clearly defined.

Generally speaking, contemporary criticism is original or contentious only within these bounds. It is permissible, for instance, to argue the pros and cons of certain ways of playing or appreciating Beethoven's last quartets, but it is nonconformist to suggest that they may not, after all, have been Beethoven's greatest works. One may accept or reject

Wieland Wagner's staging of his grandfather's music-dramas, but it is no longer good form to quarrel with the operas themselves, even if one does not happen to like them. One may prefer one contemporary composer to another, and even find fault here and there with the most famous; But it is bad form to be pessimistic about modern music, and it is a blasphemy to suggest that the road to bankruptcy began with Beethoven.

The critics of the nineteenth century used to dare this sort of dogmatic opinion, and their targets responded in kind. It made for lively exchanges of opinion. This was criticism—personal, biased, passionate and fallible. What matters who was right and who was wrong? Who can judge, even today? Are we to assume that our present view of the nineteenth century represents the ultimate and indisputably correct word on the subject? Must it be for ever binding on everyone?

Contemporary musical society conducts itself as if it assumed that the answer were yes. Contemporary criticism conforms. The existence of right and wrong in the judgment of music is acknowledged, and nobody wants to be wrong. What was right and what was wrong are held to be established. About the present one knows only that music must go on, that it must progress, that it is, indeed, progressing—however difficult it may be to applaud the evidence—and that tolerance, temperance and ambiguity are the parts of wisdom for those who sit in judgment. Such is the dogma. Its observance is plainly more dogmatic than the assertive criticism of the past, which is now denounced as dogmatism.

The result, as far as criticism is concerned, has been a droll reversal of positions as between critic and listener and as between critic and composer. Where the critic formerly aligned himself against both composer and public in defence of conservative views in which he believed passionately, he now allies himself with the composer in defence of music for which he has, at heart, little enthusiasm.

He may dislike individual compositions, and say so; but he says it politely, and more in sorrow than in anger. He will not say how bad he really thinks they are. This would expose him to the charge of being destructive. A destructive critic, according to the indulgent mores of contemporary musical society, is a villain. The critic is rather inclined to agree. He has accepted the chamber of commerce injunction: If you can't boost, don't knock.

When the composer was doing well the critic could afford to attack him, for business was healthy, and controversy was good for it. Each was immune from serious damage. The odds favoured the composer as long as he could please the public. The critic who attacked him made enemies, but he also made readers. Now, with the composer doing badly, the critic tends, as a fellow professional, to take his side. Critic and composer are dependent upon one another for survival. Neither is strong enough to withstand a series of heavy blows from the other. In effect, critic and composer are—as Virgil Thomson, in his time as critic of the *New York Herald Tribune* suggested they should be—banded together as co-professionals in a conspiracy to defend the faith.

History's disparagement of the role of the critic actually makes this change of position popular and assures for it the stamp of social approval. Today's critic is regarded as an enlightened champion of the new and the unfamiliar, the courageous defender of the composer underdog. By defending modern music in principle and occasionally disparaging it in detail he accommodates at once the superstition of progress, the distaste of the modern audience for modern music, and the requirement that he should function, from time to time, as a critic.

There is a good deal of hypocrisy in this. The critic's position is fashionable, the only one which society, with its present concept of musical history, can approve. In fact, while priding himself on his enlightenment and his courage, the critic displays little of either. It may have taken courage to defend Wagner a hundred years ago, when opposition was real and emotional. It took courage to oppose him, too, for the enthusiasts were numerous, and inspired by evangelical faith and fervour. Today it takes no courage to defend anybody, since nobody is really opposed. The contemporary critic defending modern music goes off to joust with a windmill.

He is the effete descendant of a warrior clan decimated in battle and discredited by history. His reading of the family archives had encouraged him to avoid the mistakes of his forefathers and to seek an alliance with the enemy. Since both composer and critic are aware that the arrangement is not entirely honourable, they fight a sham battle now and then to keep up appearances. But for the most part they fight together against the public—not openly under flags, but furtively, like signal-exchanging partners in a poker game.

As usual, the critic is wrong. Having seen what happened to critics who pointed out faults in composers now remembered for their virtues, he looks for virtues in composers unlikely to be remembered for any virtue at all. Or, to put it differently, the critic opposed new music when it was good, or at least when there was still good in it, and now compounds the error by defending it when there is little in it to defend.

The contemporary critic has consistently confused inspiration and inclination. As an amateur and connoisseur of European music from Bach to Bartók, he is interested in the continuity of the tradition and in making his own contribution. He has ignored as unworthy any music of different traditional origin. This has prompted him to overestimate, wishfully, uninspired new music that calls itself serious and to disparage, apprehensively, new music of less traditional physiognomy but real inspiration, notably jazz.

One might think the critic free to look for music wherever he can find it. One might expect him to enjoy the adventure of search, and rejoice in the discovery of an exciting new idiom. One is even tempted to observe that, whereas the older critics earned the opprobrium of posterity by opposing the music of their own time, it has been reserved for the critics of the twentieth century to distinguish themselves by not recognizing the music of *their* time when it was all around them.

But the temptation must be resisted. Regardless of how posterity may appraise jazz, faith in the generic superiority and the inevitable continuity of something called serious music is too vital a factor in our conventional attitudes about music; and the critic can no more escape tradition than the composer—unless, of course, he is to make a clean break and sacrifice the respect which his identification with serious music earns for him. For this, as with the composer, his equity is too great.

Since the critic, if he is to survive as anything other than a musicologist, an appraiser of performances and a chewer-of-the-cud of musical history, must have new music with which to practise living criticism and demonstrate his contemporary usefulness, he must help the composer in his effort to replenish the repertoire and support his claim of being a producer of truly modern music. He must inevitably subscribe to Mr. Thomson's "conspiracy to defend the faith".

Thus, we find composer and critic on the same side of the fence, or, to put it more accurately, seated together out on the same limb. There they are likely to stay for some time to come. Each has a saw in the form of his honest opinion of the other. But neither of them can use it without inviting his own destruction. There is no reason to expect them to indulge in any such foolishness.

PART II

# THE CRISES OF EVOLUTION IN AMERICAN MUSIC

But the denunciators of a new art or style see only that which the new art has dethroned, heretofore revered and held inviolate. They never realize that the abandonment of the means of expression, forms, and devices which are the property of a particular style is a necessity for a new style if it hopes to express the spirit of its own era; that this turning away from the traditional is a prime requisite for an art eager to give something positively new and vital. It is this new and vital that the biased critic does not see.

PAUL HENRY LANG[21]

# ACKNOWLEDGMENTS

These chapters draw upon material which appeared originally in *Jazz Quarterly* in an article entitled "Jazz and Classical"; in *High Fidelity Magazine* in articles entitled "What is This Thing Called Jazz?" and "The Beat— A New Dimension?" and in *HiFi Stereo Review* (Ziff-Davis Publishing Co., N.Y.) in articles entitled "A Slight Case of Terminology", and "Give Some Regard to Broadway".

# STATUS

THE EMERGENCE in the first half of this century of a new American musical idiom called jazz has been one of the most dramatic and exciting episodes in the history of western music.

In the short space of fifty years jazz has evolved from lowly and exotic origins in the Negro work-songs, field-hollers, blues, spirituals, gospel-songs, bar-music, marching bands and dance bands of the American South into an art music of world-wide acceptance and world-wide appeal. As a dynamic musical phenomenon it is paralleled in the history of European music only by the spread of the Italian opera idiom throughout the Continent in the eighteenth century and the spread of the German symphonic idiom throughout the Continent and beyond in the nineteenth.

The resemblances between jazz and these two principal idioms of European music, in the manner of their propagation, are striking. In each case musicians from the country of origin have taken their music abroad and enjoyed immediate, enthusiastic acceptance and imitation. Some of the musicians have remained abroad, to prosper as practitioners and teachers. Foreign musicians have come to study the new music in its native environment. In a short time it has no longer been the exclusive property of the original musicians or of the country of its origin but has been taken up and played and added to by local musicians everywhere.

Jazz most closely resembles the Italian phase in the characteristics of its evolution, if only because both idioms have represented so radical a break with tradition that a new terminology had to be found to describe their practices, conventions and purposes. The German symphonic and chamber music idiom evolved gradually from the Italian. It did not represent a radical break with tradition, and its terminology, in so far as it was German at all, was largely a translation from the Italian, which has provided for more than three centuries the basic terminology of European music, just as American English provides the basic terminology of jazz and is, indeed, the basic language of jazz musicians no matter where or by whom it is played.

Certain facts about jazz may be assumed to be established beyond question. It is today a musical idiom employed by discriminating musicians—if not, to be sure, discriminating serious musicians—and enjoyed, studied and criticized by discriminating amateurs and its own professional critics the world over. It has produced several generations of gifted, inventive and original musicians—composers, arrangers, instrumentalists and singers. It has created a new kind of orchestra and a new kind of chamber music. It has prompted a formidable and multilingual body of historical, musicological and critical literature.

In short, it cannot be dismissed as merely light or popular music, or as dance music, or as primitive folk music. The audiences at jazz concerts at Carnegie Hall in New York, the Festival Hall in London, the Kongress-Saal in Munich, the Grosser Konzerthaussaal in Vienna and the Tonhalle in Zurich—not to mention the American and European jazz festivals— are composed neither of rubes nor boobs, and their purpose in attending is neither to sing nor to dance. They come to listen, and they pay high prices for the pleasure. Such occasions are as much concerts as those of the New York, London, Berlin or Vienna Philharmonic orchestras. The music is not serious, to be sure, in the conventional sense of the term, but it is taken seriously by thousands of more or less serious-minded people, not all of them young.

This would seem to offer grounds for rejoicing. Should we not welcome this evidence that our century and our society have, indeed, made their contribution to the history of western music in the form of an idiom offering precisely what we look for in new music: freshness, originality, novelty, high standards of musicianship and virtuosity, and a following drawn, not out of a sense of duty, but rather out of a spontaneous reaction to a music that sings of its own time?

One would think that we should, but quite obviously we don't; or at least the serious musical community doesn't, and its composers, critics, practitioners and audiences are still society's unchallenged spokesmen on matters musical. It is possible and even customary in the serious musical community to write and speak about contemporary music as if there were no such thing as jazz, or as if jazz were somehow not contemporary music, or as if it were not music at all. Indeed, it is hazardous to do otherwise. The jazz idiom represents, or seems to represent, too radical a break with tradition. Its origin, growth, environment, objectives, conventions, musicians and audiences conform so little to the traditional conceptions and expectations of the serious musician and the serious musical audience that its general acceptance as an integral and major episode in the evolution of western music is, to the majority of those associated with serious music, sheerly unthinkable. Even those who recognize that it has some quality, those who are aware that there is more to it than mere pap for the vulgar, cannot imagine

it as belonging to the mainstream of the evolution of
western music.

Jazz is, for instance, an improvised music—or so one
thinks—and cannot, therefore, be compared with music
that is more or less laboriously thought out and written
down on banks of staves and is so complex that a semi-
divinity in the mortal form of a conductor is required to sort
it all out, discover its inner secrets and prepare them for
revelation. The jazz musician cannot read music—or so one
thinks. He is not dependent upon written notes in order to
be articulate, and is more or less his own composer, conductor and arranger. He cannot be compared, therefore,
with the disciplined serious musician who cannot be articulate without them, and whose purpose in life is to do just
what composer and conductor tell him to do and nothing
else. And then there are the materials, tunes, if you please
just simple melodies that anybody could write—or so one
thinks. And the instruments—blaring trumpets, sliding
trombones, squawking saxophones, obstreperous drums
and tom-toms, an electrically amplified guitar and a bass
that is slapped instead of bowed. And the audience! Young
people who chew gum in time, tap their feet and even
applaud in the middle of numbers, just as they did in
Mozart's day! Surely such a music cannot be threat to music
conceived to perpetuate the tradition of Bach, Beethoven
and Brahms!

And so the serious musical community simply closes its
ears to the disturbing new sounds. In this it is encouraged
by its leaders, particularly the critics, who themselves
ignore jazz and permit their readers the inference that what
is not worth the critics' attention is not worth their own. The
emergence of jazz in concert halls and its dissemination on

LP records have recently forced some critics (or at least some music editors) to retreat a bit, but they have done it artfully. Coverage is given to jazz in a few newspapers and periodicals, but it is usually treated separately from "music" and is left to jazz critics. Serious critics still decline to soil their ears or their reputations with it.

Thus encouraged in the wisdom, safety and respectability of ignorance, the serious-music lover has, as a rule, heard little jazz; and what he has heard will normally have been far from the best—if not the worst, or not jazz at all. In hearing whatever he has heard he has measured it against Bach, Beethoven and Brahms, listening with the expectations of one brought up on European music, and found his worst suspicions confirmed. He dismisses the matter and the music from his mind, and consoles himself about his own contemporary music with the thought that his composers, however badly they, too, may measure up against Bach, Beethoven and Brahms, at least aim high and in the right direction.

This makes it difficult to discuss jazz with serious critics, musicians and music-lovers. They will usually have heard a bit of Gershwin, a bit of rock 'n roll, and whatever American hit tunes and hill-billy trios happen to be the fad of the moment, on the world's juke-boxes or their children's gramophone records. The more sophisticated may know the names of Louis Armstrong, Duke Ellington, Benny Goodman and Count Basie, but even they are rarely more than superficially familiar with their work. One will hear derogatory opinions on jazz handed down confidently by people who have never heard a note played by Art Tatum, Teddy Wilson, Oscar Peterson, Errol Garner, Billy Taylor, Roy Eldridge, Pres Young, Johnny Hodges,

Ben Webster or Charlie Parker, or even know the names; who have never heard or heard of the Modern Jazz Quartet; who cannot tell dixieland from swing or swing from bop or are aware that they exist and that there are important distinctions between them. Under such circumstances one hardly knows where to begin.

If one is to begin at all it must be with the complex of prejudice, superstition and folklore that comprises the serious musical community's armour against the dynamism of jazz. The main bulwarks of this complex are the assumption of a generic difference between serious music and popular music, and a terminology tailored to support the assumption. Since the question of popularity, and the concept of popular music as opposed to serious music will haunt us at every step of the way in our discussion of jazz and its place in the evolution of western music, we must first examine what we mean, or ought to mean, when we talk about popularity and popular music.

If we mean success with a large public, then all the great composers were popular composers, and the greatest music of the orchestral and operatic repertoire is popular music, for most of it has enjoyed such success, and has enjoyed it in its own time. It is difficult and possibly rather uncomfortable for the serious musical community to understand that Rossini, Donizetti, Bellini, Verdi, Puccini, Meyerbeer, Gounod and Massenet were the Berlins, Kerns, Porters, Gershwins, Rodgers and Loessers of European music, if only in the sense that they enjoyed a similar popularity; but they were. Even the great German instrumental composers wrote to please a large community of listeners and were happy when they succeeded.

It was not until comparatively recently that the distinction between serious and popular music became general, unless the latter term is interpreted as referring to the crude fiddling of peasants. In the eighteenth century, as Adam Carse has put it, "the clear distinction which has grown up between 'music' and 'light music' hardly existed. . . . The most distinguished of musicians composed and took part in the performance of dance music, out-door music and music played during meals. Court orchestras were at the same time the equivalents of the modern concert-orchestra, the theatre orchestra, the dance band, the restaurant band and the open-air promenade band. The same composers wrote the music for all of them. They were not divided into sheep and goats, highbrows and lowbrows, composers of art-music and trade-music. A composer didn't lose caste when his music became popular, in fact, he gained prestige thereby and tried to make it popular."[22] In other words, the eighteenth-century composers coveted popularity, i.e. success with the public for whom they wrote and played—which, as we have noted, was by no means the small, select body of initiates sometimes pictured by impressionable critics—and the greatest of them won it by a music so exceptionally good that it set divine standards.

Ever since then composers who have associated themselves with those standards have enjoyed the warmth of the halo. In the course of the years, however, as their work showed increasing evidence of mortal labour and diminishing evidence of divine inspiration, the pretentious objective came to be valued above modest pleasure, and the original pleasurable objective was forgotten. A music that fails to give pleasure is unlikely to be popular, but since the giving of pleasure was no longer considered an admirable objective, popularity ceased to be a barometer of success, and failure to achieve it came to be regarded, if not as proof of integrity, at least as no evidence of incompetence.

At the same time, listeners of simpler tastes were catered for by composers who, while writing in the same basic idiom, were content to sacrifice immortality for popularity and its tangible rewards. Since their music remained true to the idiom, even highbrows could confess to finding pleasure in it. So long as a Brahms could say of a Strauss waltz, "Leider, nicht von Brahms," their respectability was not in danger. As produced by Suppé, Auber, Delibes, Offenbach, Bayer, Lehar, Millöcker, Johann Strauss, Oscar Strauss, Lanner, Benatzky, Friml and Herbert, it was simply a less pretentious manifestation of the same kind of music. The most pretentious composers and musicians could write it and play it, and did. Significantly it was called "light" or "semiclassical", rather than "popular", the implication being that even the pretentious can indulge in light pleasures without risking vulgarity, as long as they also remain true to their pretensions.

In the first two decades of this century, however, composers of the traditional forms of light music found themselves as unable as their more pretentious colleagues to appeal to the tastes of contemporary audiences. Unlike their colleagues they could not survive on pretensions alone, having none, and light music of the traditional European variety gradually ceased to be composed.

Here it is possibly worth noting a certain interdependence between serious and light music. In healthy times one may observe a process of exchange that works like an alternating current. From the popular terminal comes much that is vital and imaginative, uninhibited by intellectual reflection, calculation and critical appraisal. From the serious, or sophisticated terminal come flashes of invention, structural devices and refinements of syntax that often re-emerge as the clichés of the most popularly rooted music. This process takes place continuously in American indigenous music today. It was true of European music until fifty years ago when, in its most pretentious manifestations, music reached an ultimate intellectuality in the works of Schönberg and von Webern and the terminals no longer had anything in common—unless it was a shortage of vital current.

But people will have their own music. The repetition of old music, both serious and light, will satisfy some, and new serious music may satisfy others, if only because of the implied reassurance that the idiom remains alive; yet this by no means satisfies the basic social need. There was an enormous gap, and it was filled by the new indigenous American music that owed less, apparently, to Europe than to Africa and America—and the former idiomatic unity of western music was destroyed. To the music-lover brought up on European music, moreover, this was not only a new kind of music; it was the music of a new kind of society that was shaping itself—and its music—with a cheerful and careless disregard for the past and its heroes, conventions and traditions. The serious-music lover rejected it as vulgar—or popular, to use a gentler word—and the easy social and critical intercourse between serious and light music was at an end. Henceforth there would be serious music and popular music, the acceptability of the latter diminishing according to the distance it strayed from the older European models, which increased as time went on. Within a couple of decades the break was complete. Serious music became synonymous in the mind of the serious-music lover and in the mind of the general public with

E

"good" music, and popular or vulgar music became synonymous with jazz.

One would not quarrel with the association of "good" with "serious" if it were not at once so all-embracing and so exclusive. "Good" is not too much to claim for most of the European serious music that has come down to us in the standard repertoire, but it should not be applied indiscriminately to much that was left behind, nor to most of what has been contributed in the past fifty years. And the inference that only serious music can be good is monstrous. Even a majority of serious-music critics will concede that little of what has been added to its literature since the First World War has been very good, and some of them will agree that what has been contributed to popular music by jazz has been very good indeed. But as things now stand, a piece by Duke Ellington may be acknowledged to be good, but is not thought worth taking seriously, while a piece by Stravinsky may be acknowledged to be bad, but will still be thought of as better than Ellington's simply because Stravinsky writes serious or "good" music and Ellington doesn't. Terminology effects Stravinsky's—and serious music's—rescue.

Dave Brubeck and his Quartet may play a most sophisticated type of chamber music, but what they play is jazz— and therefore only popular—and they play in night clubs —and are therefore not respectable. Not even a move to Carnegie Hall will bring the serious-music critics to hear them. To be thus honoured they must play something that unites—or attempts to unite, or reconcile—jazz and serious music. In other words, in order to gain the ears of serious-music critics it is not enough that the jazz combo or jazz band move out of the night club and into the concert hall. It must come in with a symphony orchestra on its back.

A lovely example of the serious critic's point of view was afforded by Paul Henry Lang in a discussion of *Porgy and Bess* in his Sunday column of January 29, 1956, in the *New York Herald Tribune*. Mr. Lang was deploring the fact that *Porgy and Bess* is widely accepted by laymen at home and abroad as an example of American music. Foreign audiences, he wrote, are given to understand that Gershwin represents our musical art in the same sense that Milhaud represents France's or Vaughan-Williams England's.

"No one can deny," he wrote, "Gershwin's very real gifts, nor does anybody admit in public the limitations of these gifts and the fact that his music is exceptionally high quality, Broadway show-music rather than 'serious art'. . . . The very fact that we use the rather silly-sounding terms 'serious' or 'classical' music indicates that we do acknowledge the existence of some difference, and that we somehow assign a higher artistic value to, say, a symphony by Riegger or Piston than to, say, *Rhapsody in Blue* or *Showboat*."

Unfortunately, it does. A classification born of quality retains a qualitative implication for anything now written under its emblem. A symphony by Riegger or Piston is better than a suite by Ellington or a musical by Gershwin simply because it is—a symphony. The classical composer qualifies for respectability and status the moment he writes the magic word "symphony" at the top of his score. The serious-music critics, Mr. Lang at their head, persistently confuse objective and accomplishment. Curiously enough, *Porgy and Bess* was conceived as an opera and originally failed, as operas are now expected to do. It succeeded ultimately when it was found to be, not only an opera, but also a good show. So Lang dismisses a work of "exceptionally high quality" because it is "Broadway show-music rather than 'serious art'." And he dismisses *Rhapsody in Blue*, not, apparently, because it happens to be the most popular piano concerto of the past forty years, but because it is by Gershwin, a composer of Broadway show-music.

However, this kind of confusion is by no means restricted to the serious musical community. The jazz community is no longer naïve or illiterate, but it lacks the self-assurance of those to the manner born, and, like outsiders everywhere, it apes the attitudes and customs of the respectable, including the least edifying. Thus, within the jazz community today snobbery is fashionable, and of a kind that the serious musical community would probably find distasteful if it knew enough about jazz to be aware of it; for the jazz snob is the first-generation offspring of successful immigrant parents, embarrassed by their accent and manners. He is proud of their success, but ashamed of it too; for, in musical high society, to which he aspires, and which he unwittingly apes, immediate success, particularly with a general public, is looked upon with suspicion. Besides, he takes a patronizing view of a good deal of the music with which that success was earned in the past, excepting the primitives, and of almost all the music with which a similar success is being earned today. "Commercial" is the foulest epithet in his vocabulary, and it is likely to be applied to almost anyone who enjoys the following of a mass audience.

But whether proud or ashamed, depending upon his mood of the moment, the jazz snob can have it both ways. If he thinks of jazz in terms of Miles Davis, Thelonius Monk, Charles Mingus, Charlie Parker and the Modern Jazz Quartet, he may enjoy the satisfaction of belonging to a small and exclusive audience of initiates. If he thinks in terms of Louis Armstrong, Benny Goodman, Count Basie and Duke

Ellington, he can enjoy the satisfaction of a great but less
than universal popularity. If he thinks in terms of Glenn
Miller, Frank Sinatra, Bing Crosby, George Gershwin,
Cole Porter and Jerome Kern—as the serious musical
community does when it thinks of jazz—he can rub
shoulders with the masses anywhere. He can accommodate
himself to any attitude by contracting or expanding the
area of American indigenous music admissible as jazz.

This combination of confusion and ambivalence was
exemplified charmingly by André Hodeir in his book, *Jazz,
Its Evolution and Essence*, which was much admired by jazz
critics. He wrote:

"How strange have been the fortunes of this music,
which seemed destined to remain confined to the banks of
the lower Mississippi! What contemporary observer would
have guessed that the folk music of a small group would
become the language of an entire people fifteen or twenty
years later and, in a few more years, a world-wide phenomenon, with jazz bands existing simultaneously in
Melbourne, Tokyo and Stockholm. What does this success
mean? It has been said that jazz is the most fully alive form
of dance music of our time; this is true, but jazz is much
more than dance music. The importance of the movement
it has given rise to may be judged by the number of books
and magazines on the subject published all over the world.
Nothing is stranger, and nothing more reassuring for
humanity than the universal diffusion of this message first
launched by a people numbering ten million.

"We must not delude ourselves, however. Jazz has found
followers everywhere, but these followers are always in the
minority. . . . A very small number of newspapers and
magazines concerned with the arts feel it their duty to carry

a jazz column. This reticence in the face of such success and these limitations on an expansion that has been so great in other respects present a problem we cannot avoid. What are the causes of these apparent contradictions?

"At first it might seem that jazz is incapable of touching the masses and is suited only to an élite. This hypothesis would explain its limited success, but unfortunately it is contradicted by the facts. On the contrary, jazz seems to be accepted only with the greatest reservations by those regularly referred to as the élite—that is to say, the small part of the public that is capable of fully appreciating both classical and modern artistic masterpieces. . . ."[19]

Here we have, in three short paragraphs, a "world-wide phenomenon" of "universal diffusion" identified with the "limited success" of a music whose "followers are always in the minority", which might seem "incapable of touching the masses" and "be suited only to an élite". As confusing and inconsistent as this may seem to be, what Mr. Hodeir is getting at is clear enough. Whatever the success or lack of success of the serious aspects of indigenous American music, it has not been accepted in musical high society.

If "the importance of the movement it has given rise to may be judged by the number of books and magazines on the subject published all over the world", these books and magazines have not been the work of the serious-music critics. When Mr. Hodeir speaks of "limited success", he is not talking about success with an enormous world-wide audience; he is talking about the failure of jazz to achieve acceptance among those whom the world accepts as its cultural leaders. And when he speaks of a music "suited only to an élite", he is constricting his definition of jazz to a comparatively small, highly sophisticated, artistically

selfconscious and pretentious segment of American indigenous music, and his audience to an élite among the mass of
listeners around the world who have taken American indigenous music to their hearts.

A music denied acceptance by the "small part of the
public that is capable of fully appreciating both classical
and modern artistic masterpieces" creates its own élite—
but that is not enough. Self-admiration, however flattering,
is no substitute for social acceptance. As Mr. Hodeir says,
"this reticence in the face of such success, and these limitations on an expansion that has been so great in other respects
present a problem we cannot avoid".

The problem is, very simply, that there are in western
music today, and for the first time in the history of its
evolution, two distinct musical idioms and two distinct
audiences. Each idiom presents the variety of quality from
top to bottom that is common to most idioms of more or less
universal dissemination; they both also present the variety
of sophistication among their listeners that has, in the past,
been taken for granted in European music and accepted
without prejudice. One is tempted to say that the two idioms
are as different from one another as European music from
Chinese; but this would be an unwarranted exaggeration,
since jazz is too deeply rooted in European music. The
difference is, however, so great that the two audiences
regard music from different points of view, approach it
with different expectations, and experience it within the
social framework of a different complex of habits, customs
and conventions.

Comparatively few individuals among either audience are
capable of listening to the other's music with anything like
the other's understanding. They are more numerous in the

jazz than in the serious musical community, particularly among the younger generation of jazz musicians. This may be because the jazz musician and the jazz amateur, too, are more conscious of what jazz has derived and inherited from the European tradition. The serious musician and his audience, orientated towards Europe, are inclined to think of jazz as a phenomenon of Afro-American origin; they are less aware of its European antecedents and less able to relate it to their own musical experience.

Generally speaking, anyone listening to jazz from the point of view of the serious-music lover is offended by what seems to be the obviousness and obtrusiveness of the beat, the apparent insignificance of the melodies and by the absence of structural extension based upon tonal modulation. He is disturbed by an apparent want of reflective substance, or by the undignified character of such content and substance as there may be. He is adversely influenced by the infantile character of much that has been most conspicuously popular. And he is rendered sceptical by the popularity of much that has been good.

The most important of these reservations is that which has to do with the want of reflective substance. It is the reflective substance attributed to the best of European music that gives the serious musician and his audience such confidence in the superiority of the European idiom. It is the absence of this substance, or any suggestion of it, that seems to confirm them in their low opinion of jazz. The jazz musician, similarly, is awed by the intellectual glamour of serious music and disturbed by the failure of his own music to measure up to it on intellectual terms; this has recently led him to imitate serious music in an attempt to make his own music more "serious".

If then, the question of intellectual quality, or reflective substance, is the block which prevents an easy exchange of points of view, then the distance between them may be less formidable than it seems. In the long history of European music, reflective substance is associated primarily with the period dominated by the Germans. Not even then did all European music have it. But most of it, being by Germans or by composers influenced by Germans, has been associated with German intellectual characteristics.

It is with the Germans that the concept of serious music finally took hold, just as it was with the Germans that the artist, and especially the composer, came to be endowed with a kind of halo setting him off from and rather above his fellow mortals. It was the universality of German influence in the nineteenth century that led to the habit of thinking of music as serious unless specifically designated as light or popular or folk music. And it was the extraordinary quality of German music that led to the habit of considering serious music as good music, and to the perverse notion that music, in order to be good, had to be serious. The *reductio ad absurdum* is today's assumption that music seriously intended is automatically worth taking seriously.

Thus, the root problem is the qualitative association of the terminology. Musical high society still thinks of jazz as popular or vulgar music and of its followers as misguided teenagers. The world at large accepts this appraisal. Only time can resolve it. The implications inherent in a general acceptance of jazz as a music also worth taking seriously would be too tremendous for it to be otherwise. Not only musicians and critics, but also audiences would be confounded, and on both sides of the tracks. The serious musician and his audience would have to acknowledge a dynamic rival. The terminability of the European tradition would appear to be confirmed, or at least suggested. And the jazz musician and his audience would find themselves catapulted into a position of responsibility and acceptance for which they are neither musically nor psychologically prepared.

It is possible to argue that the best American indigenous music of the past thirty years has outclassed new European music and other new music written in the European idiom. But the facts remain that European music of the two preceding centuries still exerts a great fascination upon an immense international public, and also that contemporary production in the European idiom basks in the reflected glory of an older repertoire as yet unmatched by any American music. This contributes to the complacency of the serious musical community and to the awe in which this community is held even by those professionally and enthusiastically identified with American indigenous music.

To some of us the picture may seem clear enough: a glorious European tradition coming to an end, its close coinciding with the emergence of an American tradition now approaching something like maturity. But habits, customs and associations are too deeply ingrained in our collective musical thinking, and probably just as well. The implications of this picture are too momentous for too many people, and too disturbing.

The serious musician is not prepared to admit that it is all up with the music to which he has devoted his life and his affections. Nor need he do so. There will be a great audience for the masterpieces of European music for many years to come. The jazz musician, on the other hand, is hardly prepared to believe that his is really the art music of the present. He may insist that the best of it is, indeed, an art music, but he shies from the thought that it might be considered in the same breath as serious music—including contemporary serious music—for he is as much a victim of the folklore of musical appreciation as anyone else. He cannot escape the impact of the halo cast by such names as Bach, Beethoven, Brahms, Verdi, Wagner, Strauss, Debussy, Ravel and Stravinsky. Because of Beethoven he hesitates to compare Ellington with von Webern or Pierre Boulez, although the evidence of his ears may suggest that what Ellington has written is music and what von Webern and Boulez have written is not.

We may expect no sudden changes in society's attitudes towards these two musical idioms. Jazz will doubtless continue to be regarded, patronizingly, as popular, regardless of its quality, and new music conceived as serious will continue to be taken seriously, regardless of its sterility or essential triviality. That music can be worth taking seriously without being serious is unlikely to be acknowledged by musical high society as it exists today or will exist for many years. This would be a matter of indifference if only musical high society alone were affected. The element of tension derives from the jazz musician's desire to be taken seriously. If he persists in the notion that respectability and status can be acquired by studied originality, eccentricity, defiance of his listeners and the composition of twelve-tone jazz, he will be ruined before his time has come.

# DEFINITION

OUR DISCUSSION SO FAR will have made it clear that
not everyone who talks about jazz is talking about the
same thing.

We have noted that most serious musicians, serious
critics and serious-music lovers, when they talk about jazz,
refer to the main body of American popular music, and
usually to the least distinguished part of it. They will rarely
have heard anything else.

A part of the problem is, of course, the fact that the kinds
or styles of jazz which have been most widely popular, and
of which society as a whole has been most acutely aware,
have almost always been a white dilution or adaptation of a
Negro original. There could not otherwise have been such
a universal dissemination or acceptance. But this has
encouraged the knowledgeable and the discriminating to
denounce what is commonly understood to be jazz as "not
the real thing".

When people talked about jazz in the twenties, for
instance, they were thinking, not about King Oliver and
Louis Armstrong's Hot Five, but about Paul Whiteman,
Vincent Lopez, Ben Bernie and Ted Lewis and the songs of
George Gershwin and Irving Berlin. Paul Whiteman was
known in those days as "the King of Jazz". The first book
on jazz in the United States, Henry Osgood's *So This Is
Jazz*, published by Little Brown in 1926, did not mention
the name of a single Negro musician. In a book on jazz
today one will hardly find the names of Whiteman, Lopez,

Bernie or Lewis, unless the author is discussing some now famous musician who, in his early days, was so down on his luck that he was reduced to playing with them. "Bix" Beiderbecke playing with Paul Whiteman is the classic example.

In the following decade, few of the fans who proclaimed Benny Goodman as "the King of Swing" had heard or were aware of the earlier Negro big bands of Jimmie Lunceford, Fletcher Henderson, Benny Moten and Count Basie. Even more recently, at the height of the rock 'n roll craze, few of its enthusiasts, or even of its critics, were aware of the parent rhythm-and-blues, which had been the popular music of the American Negro for twenty years or more.

In other words, while jazz criticism now tends to think of jazz in terms of what was contributed to it by two or three generations of superbly original Negro musicians in New Orleans, Kansas City, Chicago and New York, and by those white musicians who were most closely identified with them, the rest of the world (including the serious musical community) knows little of all this. It has always thought of jazz in terms of less radically original, more readily assimilable white derivatives in which European influences are more obviously and more decisively at work.

And then there is the adjacent problem: the functions of jazz. The jazz musician and the jazz critic do not think of jazz as dance music, and do not want to. Admittedly, there is no dancing at jazz concerts or in night clubs where jazz bands and jazz combos are the principal attraction; but the facts remain that all the great bands of jazz history, including those of today, have played for dancing, and that just about every dance band in the world today that is not a Latin-American band, plays jazz, or something like it, or tries to.

Another important problem concerns the musical material of jazz. Jazz musicians and jazz critics, dissociating their music from popular music, refuse to consider Irving Berlin, George Gershwin, Cole Porter and other American song-writers as jazz musicians or composers; but it is impossible to deny that the American popular song, even more than the revered blues, has provided the jazz musician's basic melodic and harmonic materials. Not for nothing are the famous songs of these composers referred to in discussions of jazz repertoire as "standards".

A good example of this confusion is the following extract from Vernon Duke's *Passport to Paris*. Duke is speaking of the impression made upon him by Gershwin's "Swanee" when he first heard it in Constantinople in 1920:

"The bold sweep of the tune, its rhythmic freshness, and especially its syncopated gait, hit me hard, and I became an 'early jazz' fiend. That's not quite what I mean, because (shudder, ye New Orleans purists!) the 'real' New Orleans jazz and the true-blue blues impressed me considerably less. . . . I wanted to acquire the knack of writing popular tunes in the American idiom. The purist will tell you haughtily that it's not jazz at all—so be it; if 'Tea for Two' 'The Man I Love', 'Night and Day' and—forgive the plug—my own 'I Can't get Started With You' are not jazz, you can have all the 'Tiger Rags' in the world and welcome."[20]

This confusion becomes chaotic when one discusses the people who sing these songs. Ella Fitzgerald, Billie Holiday and Sarah Vaughan, all Negroes, are commonly accepted as jazz singers by jazz critics, despite their successes as singers of popular music. This is understandable in view of their long association with jazz as it is understood, however vaguely, by jazz musicians. But what is one to say when a jazz critic announces that he considers Bing Crosby and Frank Sinatra to be jazz singers?

They have the rhythmic feeling for it, he says, and the gift of free melodic articulation that is the essence of jazz. Ralph J. Gleason, jazz critic of the *San Francisco Chronicle*, reviewing Bing Crosby's autobiographical book, *Call Me Lucky*, went so far as to say: "Bing is the personification of the whole jazz movement—the relaxed, casual, natural and uninhibited approach to art."

Jazz musicians, jazz critics and jazz fans persist, nevertheless, in claiming a distinction between jazz and popular music, although no two of them are likely to agree as to just what the distinction is or where the line is to be drawn. According to André Hodeir's comments, mentioned previously, they also tend to expand or contract the area of music admissible as jazz depending upon whether they wish to stress its popularity or its exclusiveness.

But these are only the more obvious problems of definition. Let us listen for a moment to men whose status as jazz musicians is unquestioned, even by the jazz critics, and note how they talk about each other and about what they think jazz is—or isn't.

Here, for instance, is the bassist, Charles Mingus, speaking about the pianist, Oscar Peterson, and the clarinettist, Buddy de Franco in a blindfold test in the American jazz periodical, *Downbeat*: "No stars! Because this is supposed to be a jazz review, and I don't think that's jazz."

Here is Mingus again on the modern saxophonist, Lee Konitz: "This makes me mad, because it's not jazz, and people are calling this kind of beat jazz. Dave Brubeck gets

the same beat . . . I think these cats hate jazz !" Said Mingus
of the modern drummer, Shelly Manne: "Since he left
Kenton, he's found out what jazz is."

At about the same time that this *Downbeat* interview
occurred, one could find in *Metronome*, a rival periodical,
Shelly Manne (who now knows what jazz is) describing "the
exciting exploration emanating from . . . Dave Brubeck",
and the modern arranger, Pete Rugolo, speaking of Oscar
Peterson "taking chorus after chorus, even on the blues,
and really building, really getting somewhere".

In the same periodicals one will find Stan Kenton saying
that the Glenn Miller band "was not a jazz band, ever !"
and John S. Wilson, jazz critic of the *New York Times*,
saying of Kenton: "Any view of the merit of his band is
conditioned by the extent to which the listener will go along
with Kenton's notion that either shrieking brass or dolorous
solemnity are indicative of advanced jazz."

All this has to do with jazz of relatively recent date.
There are those who would define jazz as that music which
ended with swing, in other words, with the big bands which
came into vogue in the late twenties and early thirties. But
even so-called traditional jazz is not uniformly defined. We
find Billy Taylor, a serious student as well as one of the
most admired of modern jazz pianists, in his booklet,
*Dixieland Solos and How To Play Them*, saying: "Though
it featured syncopation and some improvisation, Dixieland
was not jazz. It was a new way of playing, not a new
music."

Jazz, then, is a new music, not a new way of playing. But
how does one reconcile this with the statement of a veteran
jazz critic who, when asked if most popular music today
were not more or less derived from jazz, said: "Not at all.

Jazz is not really a music, it's a way of playing?" Then contrast this with the statement of another veteran jazz critic: "Dixie has passed from the status of a specialized esoteric jazz into a new acceptance as popular music. . . . Similarly one can hear swing music, such as the bands of the thirties provided, on any major TV show today."

An old-timer, a great name in the jazz world, complained that the modern jazz musicians were ruining jazz. This was passed on to a modern jazz musician, whose comment was: "I have news for ——! What he's playing is rhythm-and-blues!" This, as we have noted, is the term for the Negro forerunner of rock 'n roll, which is despised and rejected by jazz musicians, although a great many of them have played one or the other, and some of them are spoken of as having "graduated" from them to jazz. An American jazz and popular record producer once said: "We are frequently called upon to explain rhythm-and-blues to people who 'confuse' it with jazz. Our answer is simply this: There is no definable difference and never has been. . . . Historically, jazz and rhythm-and-blues have been one."

The foregoing may suffice to demonstrate the confusion, even among those close to the subject, regarding what it is people are talking about when they talk about jazz. Indeed, confusion is greater among those close to the subject than among others, if only because they know enough to know how far from simple it all is.

But somehow the mere recitation of these problems, or of these aspects of the single problem of definition, seems to suggest a solution, or at least an approach to a solution. When people talk about jazz, whether about what it is or what it is not, they are talking about American music. It is American music, not just because Americans write it, or improvise it, or arrange it, or play it, but because it has evolved in all its various phases and styles in response to the various tastes of the various segments of the American musical public—excluding, of course, the serious musical public. Whatever one calls it, or whatever one calls any aspect or part of it, there can be no question but that it is distinctively, indigenously American.

Friedrich Gulda, the Austrian pianist who once followed up a recital of Beethoven sonatas in Carnegie Hall by sitting in with the Modern Jazz Quartet at Birdland, has put it this way:

"I would agree in principle that indigenous American music must be regarded as an entity. The question of what derives from what, however, is almost unanswerable, since the various trends and directions continually overlap. . . . One thing is certain, namely, that jazz is the best part of American music. With this qualification, one can recognize the totality of American music, distinguishing between good, bad and indifferent in the time-honoured manner. In other words, the spirit of American music is the same throughout, but it is at its purest in jazz."

This is a view with which a good many jazz musicians and jazz critics—although certainly not all—might agree. It would seem that the jazz musician, seeking to avoid a prejudicial classification of himself as a merely popular or commercial musician, identifies himself with that element of American music which has been, unquestionably, the most original and the most inventive, namely, the contribution of the Negro jazz musician. There is, indeed, every reason why the conscientious musician should be eager to associate himself with so obviously superior a model. But in doing so he tends to overlook the extent to which the

Negro influence has already affected almost every aspect of American indigenous musical expression. As Leonard Feather has said of Louis Armstrong, "He lives in a lot of the music you hear on commercial radio programmes; his influence can be felt, and the phrases and ideas he developed can be heard in music that is far removed from jazz." The jazz musician also tends to overlook the European contribution to even that music most closely associated with the Negro.

It would seem, then, that the most promising approach to the problem of definition might be an attempt to determine what it is that sets off American music from European music rather than an obviously doomed attempt to draw the border between jazz and popular. I would suggest that we begin with the fact that jazz has produced a new and distinctive type of musician.

We may grant at the outset that a number of serious musicians can play jazz and that many jazz musicians can play serious music, although it should be added that this is generally limited on both sides to musicians of the younger generation. The fact remains that rarely, if ever, is a musician equally effective or equally at home in both fields. Most musicians will agree that two separate and distinct frames of technical and expressive reference are involved.

This difference in frame of reference would seem to be something new in western music. In former times serious music has been distinguished from light music or folk music by higher aesthetic aspirations, by greater structural complexity and larger formal dimensions, by superior melodic and harmonic invention, and by the more exacting technical and interpretive demands imposed upon the executant. But rhetoric and syntax were basically the same.

There was nothing about light music that the best musicians could neither comprehend nor execute, and it was possible, as with a Johann Strauss, for light music of exceptional quality to achieve artistic canonization.

Granted, if one were to be guided solely by the written notes, it would be possible to conclude that the present situation as between jazz and serious music represents no radical departure from the earlier pattern as between serious and light. Notation and basic structure of composition remain essentially unchanged, although jazz, in elaborating upon the conventional thirty-two bar melody, usually confines itself to the theme and variation form. When jazz is written down, any serious musician can read it and play it, i.e. he can play the notes and he can play them in the tempo indicated. But what he produces, unless he happens to be versed in both fields, will not be jazz.

This is not satisfactorily rationalized by the assumption that the jazz musician, playing the same notes in the same tempo, would add to them improvisationally, and that this element of improvisation would represent the difference between his performance and that of the serious musician. The jazz musician would play the same notes without improvisation and still produce a fundamentally different music. The serious musician could improvise and still not produce jazz.

There must be, then, a difference untranslatable into written notation, unreflected in the printed score. That there is such a difference has long been acknowledged. Some have attempted to isolate jazz as an African music, but the argument, if such it may be called, breaks down before the fact that there is no jazz in Africa that was not brought there by Americans or Europeans. Others have stressed improvisation, but, as we have just noted, the serious musician can improvise without producing jazz; moreover, improvisation was an essential element of European music until about a century ago. But usually the distinction is sought in rhythm. Jazz is described as a music of rhythm, and the jazz musician's superiority in his own idiom is ascribed to his peculiar rhythmic sense. There is truth in this, but it leaves much still unexplained.

Jazz would seem, at first glance, to be rhythmically simpler than serious music. The written notes show the same four beats to the bar familiar to the serious musician as "common time". In this respect, serious music, with its variety of simple and compound rhythmic patterns and its dynamic resources of rubato, accelerando, ritardando, etc., would seem, on paper at least, to offer a greater emphasis on rhythm and a greater rhythmic variety. Nor does the familiar description of jazz as a syncopated music get us any further. Written-down jazz will show no device of syncopation not familiar in serious music. If syncopation were the answer, then much serious music would be jazz.

But let us return for a moment to our two musicians—let us say they are pianists—one serious, the other jazz. Let us see what happens when each of them plays a piece of written-down jazz. And let us look as well as listen. The eye will at once pick up an important difference. The jazz musician will beat the rhythm with his foot. The serious musician, not versed in jazz, will not.

To the serious musician this habit of beating time with the foot—or, for that matter, with the drum or double bass— is one of the repulsive aspects of jazz. It seems to imply a want of true rhythmic sensibility, certainly a lack of rhythmic subtlety. It suggests a kind of elementary stage of musical development, associated in the mind of the serious musician with the beginner counting out loud.

The jazz musician's view is quite another. To him the explicit beat is what sends him aloft and keeps him there. It supports his rhythmic, melodic and harmonic flight. He can be with it, ahead of it, behind it or against it. As long as it is there with him, and he with it; as long as his relationship to it is secure, easy and relaxed, he is, so to speak, musically airborne. If he were to lose contact with it, or if he were to come into uncontrolled conflict with it, he would come plummeting back to earth.

Basically, this is what is implied by the term, "swing", certainly a more communicative word than "jazz". It is a commonplace of jazz jargon that a musician who is thought to swing is considered a jazzman, and that one who does not swing is not. Swinging is, after all, a kind of flying. And the essence of jazz is musical flight, sustained by rhythmic pulsations.

This is, of course, more or less true of all music, and the discovery of some jazz critics that certain serious musicians sustain themselves, rhythmically, better than others has led them to suggest that these musicians swing. It must be plain, however, that such swinging, if it can, indeed, be called that, is mild compared with the jazz musician's flight. It is probably not too much to say that from the jazz musician's point of view, much serious music, and especially music written or influenced by the German symphonists, however admirable, can seem comparatively earthbound.

The dramatic, reflective and recitative character of nineteenth-century serious music exacted a price in rhythmic debility. The dynamic faculty of tempo changes, both sudden and gradual, and all the dramatic inflection inherent

in various types of acceleration and retardation, contributed
to the weakening of the beat as a phenomenon collectively
anticipated and collectively experienced. Where more than
a few were gathered together, as in an orchestra, a conductor
was required to determine it, to make it explicit and to
regulate it. But not even in the eighteenth century, nor
in the waltzes, polkas and marches of a later day, did the beat
have the propulsive force that it has in jazz today, nor had
the musician the same easy, rocking relationship to it.

Some jazz musicians prefer to define jazz in terms of
phrasing rather than in terms of the beat. And there is some
help in this, since it points up the interdependence of beat
and melodic line. Certainly it is not the beat alone that makes
jazz. Military bands produce an explicit beat, but the
marches they play are not jazz. It is the beat and the blowing,
singing or playing musician's unique relationship to it. It is
this relationship that produces the jazz phrase. It is here,
rather than in any attempt at a definition of the jazz beat
as distinct from the beat in serious music—granting that the
one is explicit and regular, the other usually implicit and
subject to calculated irregularity—that one may hope to
arrive at an appreciation of the rhythmic character of jazz.
In no other western music has the beat been so essentially
explicit and propulsive, or the musician's relationship to
whatever beat is present so organically secure, relaxed and free.

Thus, while it is probably correct to describe the difference between jazz and serious (between American and
European) as essentially rhythmic, it is important to comprehend the nature of the rhythmic difference. It is not a
question of difference in the counting of bars, or even in the
fashioning of rhythmic patterns. It is not a question of
syncopation, or of any other rhythmic device. It is rather a

question of the explicit beat as a supporting structural force and the jazz musician's assiduous and calculated exploitation of its propulsive faculties.

His failure to grasp this may explain the serious musician's tendency to regard jazz not only as basically rhythmic, but also as rhythmically inferior, bound to the beat, and lacking in sophistication, subtlety and refinement. From the jazz musician's point of view the beat is not rhythmically restrictive, but rather rhythmically liberating. Instead of being governed in his melodic progress by a pattern of counts and their exactly calculated fractional sub-divisions, he is propelled and sustained by highly charged impulses. Thus sustained, he can be rhythmically free without being out of time.

True, his music may be written and felt in a four-to-the-bar pattern, and he may count it accordingly; his melodies may be constructed in orderly eight-bar periods. But the regularity and force of the beat permit and support a freedom of melodic flight denied to his serious colleague. When the classical musician deviates rhythmically, he takes the beat with him. When the jazz musician deviates, the beat remains where he left it, an explicit point of rhythmic reference, and his deviation becomes a source of structural tension.

This liberating function of the beat is not always understood, even by jazz musicians, who sometimes talk of breaking the "tyranny of the beat"—and sometimes even try to. In this they remind us of the serious composer rebelling against the restraints of tonality. The one denies himself the effects of suspense and relief, unrest and repose, tension and release, that serious composers have traditionally derived from exposing tonal equilibrium to calculated jeopardy; the other denies himself the same effects, which he has traditionally derived from exposing rhythmic equilibrium to calculated jeopardy. In either case, by denying either tonality or the beat, the musician destroys the equilibrium without which there can be no jeopardy, no structural tension and—in the end—no structure and no song.

In spite of such rebels, it is, I believe, the explicit beat and the jazz musician's swinging relationship to it that distinguishes jazz—and, to a greater or less degree, most American music—from European music. It is what gives to American music the special character that leads most people not closely identified with the subject to think of American popular music as jazz, whether the music be Lombardo or Basie, Whiteman or Ellington, Duchin or Tatum, Gershwin or John Lewis, Presley or Ella Fitzgerald.

There are many differences among the many varieties of American music, some of them fundamental. These are often the differences that prompt emotional discussions among the initiates about what is jazz and what is not. But one thing all varieties have in common: they work from and with the beat in a way that European music never did. They may not all work from it in precisely the same way. But without it a Lombardo would collapse as inevitably as a Basie.

If I am correct in my assessment of this indigenous American music as bearing the mainstream of western musical evolution in this century, then it would seem possible that the role played by the explicit beat in determining the character of this music may be comparable to that played by the new diatonic harmony when polyphony gave way to accompanied monody in European music at the beginning of the seventeenth century.

This transition from polyphonic to a harmonically supported monodic music was the most drastic occurrence in the history of European music after organum. It determined the course of European musical evolution for three hundred years. Polyphonic invention and structure had become too complex, too elaborate and too artificial: it had become too far removed from song.

That has also been the infirmity of European music and other music based on European models in the past fifty years. And again we find a new idiom pushing its way up from the roots of song, this time with a new concept of rhythm rather than a new concept of harmony as the revitalizing element. In neither case—neither in the new Italian music of the seventeenth century, nor in the new American music of the twentieth—was the old art suddenly thrown overboard. There was plenty of polyphony in Europe's three-hundred-year monodic-harmonic period, and there is plenty of harmony in the new American period, which the future may well classify as the rhythmic, or pulsative, period of western musical evolution.

In each case—or in each evolutionary phase—we have had an amalgam of the same elements. That is, we have had melody, rhythm and a system for the organization of multiple-voiced music. And in each phase one of these elements has been dominant to the extent that it determined the character of the music of the epoch, establishing the paramount effective frame of reference for the musician's structural and expressive purpose.

Many thoughtful musicians, both jazz and serious, have recognized the pulsative element as the distinctive feature of indigenous American music without, however, grasping the full implications of the distinction. An instructive example was the appreciation of the jazz drummer's function contributed to the April, 1956, issue of *High Fidelity Magazine* by Harold Farberman, percussionist of the Boston Symphony Orchestra. Calling attention to the importance to the serious percussion section, and to the serious composer, of the contributions to the art of percussion made by the jazz drummer, Mr. Farberman wrote:

"The jazz drummer has introduced new techniques. He has demanded and received better instruments. He has developed a new and revolutionary rhythmic style, what jazzmen call 'swinging'. The classical drummer could profit from attention to the rhythm and phrasing of the better jazz drummers—Don Lamond, Louis Bellson, Art Blakey, Max Roach, Shelly Manne and Kenny Clark

"The jazz and/or dance drummer is, I should make clear, not what I have in mind as the optimum future classical percussionist. Yet a useful present step for the modern composer and classical percussionist would be to absorb some of the essence of jazz drumming, because the jazz drummer plays within his organization and is at the pulsating heart of it. Most serious composers, on the other hand, seem to write percussion parts as an afterthought and, therefore, they generally write for percussion outside the inner fabric of the music.

"The core of the general failure of American (serious) composers thus far to write creatively for percussion lies in their inability to write with pulsation, not only for percussion, but in their writing for the whole orchestra. The rhythms (and the harmonic and melodic material they accompany) that have come out of America in jazz and in many of the folk musical idioms are missing in most American classical writing. The reason is that most American composers are influenced by and try to emulate their European elders (who are, in many cases, their teachers, since nearly all the prominent American composers have studied in Europe).

"Gershwin, who has been very much underrated, *did* have the ability to convey this American rhythmic feeling. He was able to infuse his music with a feeling akin to that which exists when a good musician improvises in a jazz vein. . . . But most other American composers have a basically European conception of American music, it seems to me. The source material the American composer should most intensively investigate and experience now is American jazz. The work of the best jazzmen, to judge from its percussion content, has much of value for the serious composer in search of new modes of expression. In a score he cannot, of course, simulate an improvised Louis Armstrong or Charlie Parker solo, but he can incorporate into his writing a degree of the *feeling* of improvised jazz and, to some extent, he can incorporate the way the jazzman phrases and the way he selects his notes.

"The American composer, if he wants to catch his rhythm for himself, must naturally first go to the pulsating source, learn more about percussion, particularly the varied art of the jazz drummers. When he is able to capture the 'swing' of American jazz in his writing for the whole orchestra —including percussion—then the legendary and much-joked-about 'American Symphony' may finally come to life."

This excerpt is worth quoting at length because it is so illustrative of the failure of even those serious musicians who sense the qualities of jazz to understand how good it is or what is implied by the emergence of a good music foreign to their own experience and musical expectations. It is, in a word, an example of enlightened—or at least not entirely benighted—complacency. Mr. Farberman obviously recognizes the musician's swinging relationship to an explicit beat as the distinctive element of jazz. His comparison of the jazz drummer playing *within* his organization with the classical composer writing for percussion "outside the inner fabric of the music" is wonderfully acute. It is the same with his observation that American composers have "a basically European conception of American music". And he is shrewder than most jazz musicians in noting that Gershwin "*did* have the ability to convey this American rhythmic feeling". But he spoils it all by the reference to jazz as "source material" and the statement: "When he [the American serious composer] is able to capture the 'swing' of American jazz in his writing for the whole orchestra —including percussion—then the legendary and much-joked-about 'American Symphony' may finally come to life."

This reflects, of course, the standard view of jazz as a folk music available to the serious composer for processing into some higher form of musical art. It also identifies the higher musical art with the symphony, a European form and a European concept. It seems to assume that the American serious composer, by incorporating a swinging beat or pulsation into the symphonic form, can achieve an American serious music. I consider this very unlikely. By introducing swing into the symphony he will simply be doing what the jazzman does better with his own orchestra, and he will also be introducing an element incompatible with the character, purposes and traditions of the symphony. In order to capture the "swing" of American jazz the serious composer would have to eliminate most of the symphony orchestra. It would get in his way. In other words, he will have to write jazz, or—granting that jazz cannot be written —he will have to write in a style susceptible to the jazz idiom of performance, and he will have either to write for jazz musicians or make jazz musicians out of serious musicians. The two idioms are irreconcilable.

If these thoughts and observations about the definition of jazz are reasonably pertinent, then it must be clear that the term should be more liberally applied than jazz musicians and critics have heretofore been disposed to apply it; and more earnestly employed than the serious musicians and critics have been wont to employ it. Almost all indigenous American music has the beat, more or less, and the performer's relaxed, swinging relationship to it, whether the specific idiom be ragtime, traditional jazz, swing, bop, rhythm-and-blues, rock 'n roll, gospel singing, country and western or the songs and dances of the musical. It is this quality of free swinging, with its invitation to free melodic variation, elaboration and invention, that has proved so attractive and has caused this American music to be loved and imitated all over the world. It is an uninhibited music in a world and particularly in a youth longing for freedom of expression and behaviour. Its pulse reflects the restless and inexorable momentum of the pace of modern urban life, and its lean and pithy structures a characteristic lack of concern for non-essentials—including any suggestion of intellectual baggage and reflective complication. This may offend the serious musician, but it should not persuade him to overlook a modern musical production of such vitality.

All this applies, as I have attempted to demonstrate, to a lot more American music than is acknowledged by the jazz musician as jazz. It is, of course, no more than a wishful thought, but a tempting one, namely, that we might drop the term "jazz" and think instead of an indigenous American music already well on the way to becoming the characteristic music of the twentieth century. Even the most finicky jazz musician will agree that the inventions of the Armstrongs, Goodmans, Ellingtons and Basies have become the clichés of the run-of-the-mill commercial product. But he forgets, while deploring this dilution or commercialization, that it is proof of an accomplishment more momentous than a hundred minor masterpieces: the creation of a style, a set of conventions born of contemporary taste, mutually agreed to and understood by musicians and their listeners. It is something that has been missing from serious music for the better part of this century. Style is the prerequisite for communication, good or bad. Without a style accepted by musicians and listeners alike, the contemporary composer has been unable to communicate. With a style, mutually recognized and mutually understood, the jazz musician has communicated in every degree of quality and without restriction to national or ethnical boundaries.

If one accepts this idea of an American style one is tempted to suggest that we might better think of musical life today in terms of American music and European music rather than in the more usual and, as we have seen, both inadequate and inaccurate terms of jazz and classical, or popular and serious. The division would not be as radical as it might at first appear, for both categories, or idioms, exist within the evolutionary arch of western music, and jazz itself is more deeply rooted in Europe than in America. Indeed, I like to think of it as a continuation or extension of the European tradition born of the collision between

primitive Africa and cultivated Europe on American soil.
A Europe no longer possessed of any untapped primitive
sources, found in the United States the essential reminder
that music springs from the heart rather than the head, and
expresses itself in song and rhythm, no matter how wonderfully it may be ultimately refined and enriched by the mind.
It is a phenomenon worth the reflection of every musical
historian, musicologist and critic, that America's great
contribution to the evolution of western music was made
originally by men who could not read music.

In attempting to place jazz in the evolutionary arch of
western music it is important to remember that America
itself is essentially an extension of Europe upon a new
continent, and that no element of American culture is
completely free of European influence or tradition. American music, or jazz, is more European than African, even
though it may be the African whom he must thank for
those qualities and characteristics which most distinguish it
from European. That it has proven to be so attractive to
Europeans is evidence that it speaks for the contemporary
European as well as for the contemporary American, just as
Italian music in the seventeenth and eighteenth centuries
spoke for Germans and Frenchmen and Englishmen as
well as for Italians. Of the basic relationship to the European
tradition there can be no doubt, despite the irreconcilability
of the two idioms. And there is progress, too, if we think of
progress in terms of movement and change and growth
rather than in terms of improvement. No one will argue that
even the best of American music is an improvement upon
Bach, but neither, for that matter, is the music of Schönberg
or Bartók; and it would appear to be the sheerest idiocy to
dismiss it as worthless simply because Bach is better. What

is important to our purpose in seeking insight into the crisis of evolution in western music is not a Bach or a Beethoven but a music that is truly of our time.

This we have. Conventional musical criticism has overlooked it because it emerged in an unlikely quarter and found its audience outside that public which fancies itself to be musically sophisticated. The musical intellectuals looked for a musical art, already too intellectual, to continue developing in accordance with requirements levied by themselves, and it has never occurred to them to question their own credentials as arbiters of what is music and what is not. For them now to admit the contemporary sovereignty of a music of humble, naïve origin which, so far as they have been aware of it, they have despised, would be to confess a critical bankruptcy unprecedented in the history of western music. We need not expect them to do it.

A younger generation of critics is already beginning to appreciate the qualities of this music that their elders so gaily dismissed. This generation preserves the faith in the continuity of serious music, to be sure, but it has heard the Modern Jazz Quartet and is beginning to ask itself some searching questions. A third generation, to whom the facts may be less horrifying, should be able to see the picture in perspective and elucidate it without defensive bias.

Probably the situation will remain confused for another two or three generations. Serious music will continue to have a vast audience, and among this audience many will be reluctant to concede that the music they enjoy is unlikely to be enriched by any further masterpieces. The audience for American music will continue to be divided into factions more aware of the divergencies than the similarities among such specific idioms as traditional jazz, swing, bop, rock 'n

F

roll, country and western, the American musical, and popular tunes and passing gimmicks. There are, as we have seen, many obstacles in the way of clarification. There is no need to review them. But one of them is the term "jazz", itself, an ugly and undignified word. Unfortunately, it cannot be done away with. But this obstacle could be removed if we were to acknowledge that what confronts us in music today is a new American tradition, derived from jazz, inseparable from jazz, and of which, as Mr. Gulda has put it, jazz is still the best part. As to what constitutes the best part, that is quite obviously more a matter of opinion than of definition. What we have been attempting to define is American music.

# THE MUSICAL THEATRE

IT SHOULD BE superfluous to emphasize the kindred relationship of music and theatre. European music, of the kind known to us as serious music, was born, as we have noted, in the Italian theatre of the seventeenth century, and most of the greatest composers of European music since then have written for the theatre. Even medieval music, centred on the church, served a dramatic purpose. Nor is it just a European phenomenon. The relationship has been demonstrated in other civilizations, from the most primitive to the most advanced.

Although I have elsewhere defined opera as the musical or lyrical extension of the theatre, one might also argue that in the beginning there was music and that, if poetry is the lyrical extension of speech, and music the lyrical extension of poetry, then the theatre is the representational extension of song. The argument would seem difficult to support against the evidence to the contrary provided by the contemporary theatre, which makes little use of music, as a rule, and hardly more of poetry. But that may be part of what is wrong with the theatre. It has not been so many years since most playwrights were poets, and actors delivered their verses in a style that was closer to song than to speech. Nor should we forget that for much of Europe opera and theatre have been synonymous and that the finest playwrights and poets wrote opera libretti.

Music and drama both proceed from the impulse to achieve a concentration and sublimation of life-experience, something more than merely an exact representation, repetition or replica. This "more" is, almost by definition, a distortion, artificial in the sense that it represents a calculated and artistically purposeful departure from reality, whose details are magnified, diminished or ignored as required to accommodate the artist's communicative and structural purpose. Music represents a distortion of the cadences of speech, and theatre a distortion of the dramatic situations in human relationships. The basic musical form is a song, essentially a narrative seeking sublimation through the dramatic faculties of the voice, lyrically sustained. The basic form of the theatre is similarly a narrative, acted out and seeking sublimation through the lyrical and dramatic faculties of gesture and voice. Gesture, lyrically extended, leads ultimately to dance or choreography. The voice, lyrically extended, leads ultimately to song, or musical composition. The theatre gains by recourse to the dramatic accents of music and dance, and music by the graphic and dynamic presence of actors. The two are never entirely separate, however great the variety of proportion in any given musical or theatrical composition. Even in the play without music there is music in the speech of the actors, and even in the purely musical composition there is drama in the climaxes and cadences of musical structure. Between these "pure" forms and the ultimate of integration achieved, for instance, in the operas of Wagner and Verdi there can be and has been an infinite variety in the distribution of responsibilities, in the ratio of music to drama and vice versa, in every imaginable musical and theatrical form.

This is all as true today as it was in the time of the Greeks or in the time of Gluck and Mozart or of Wagner and Verdi. It speaks for the critical bankruptcy of our generation that the contemporary medium in which it has been most triumphantly and pleasurably demonstrated, namely, the American musical, has been ignored by music critics (including jazz critics), and slighted by dramatic critics, in whose province, by the perverse tradition of American and British journalism, it falls.

Like jazz (accepting, for the moment, the jazz musician's narrower definition of the term), the American musical has been handicapped in achieving recognition and status by its lowly origin and by the enormous popularity of its outstanding productions—a popularity ranging from the hundreds of thousands who may see a show in the theatre to the millions who may see the film version and to the many more millions who may listen to, play or sing its most engaging numbers without ever having seen it either on the stage or in a cinema.

This kind of success is not among the criteria that engage the benevolent attention of critics, dramatic or musical. The music critic is no longer concerned with mere song, and the constant production of good songs does not prompt him to honour the composer with his personal attention. Even the jazz critic tends to dismiss song, except for the sacrosanct blues, as the more or less incidental raw material for the jazz improvisation or arrangement; nor is he much impressed by a kind of music and a kind of performance more deeply rooted in European models than the kind of American music which he admires as jazz. And the dramatic critic, while he has dealt with the American musical theatre more fairly than could have been expected of music critics, has not taken it seriously, either as music or theatre. Like music critics, he looks for and is impressed with a more conspicuous, a more studied, a more radical and a more pretentious kind of originality. The evolution of the American musical theatre from the light opera and revue of the twenties to the mature "musical" of the fifties has been normal and gradual, and fortunately free from the kind of purposeful eccentricity that calls attention to itself as modern art—whether musical, theatrical or graphic. In a medium such as a musical, which looks for a return on so vast an investment, there is fortunately no place for the odd ball.

Also like jazz, the American musical represents such a variety of influences, with the proportions of one to the other varying so greatly from show to show, that it is hard to define and, therefore, to classify. The two thousand odd productions of the past fifty years have answered to such designations as light opera, operetta, musical comedy, extravaganza, revue, musical show and just plain musical. In the course of the last decade the last of these has begun to emerge as the accepted generic term, but still, within the standard two-act format of the musical, there is a great and confusing variety of types of show, ranging from the conspicuously American idiomatic *Guys and Dolls* to the conspicuously light operatic later shows of Rodgers and Hammerstein.

What makes it possible now to speak of "the musical" generally is the extent to which any of the newer shows is unmistakably American regardless of the recipe. One may think of such a piece as *The King and I* as essentially light opera, but one could never suspect that it was the work of Léhar or Benatzky, or even of Romberg or Friml. Too many distinctively American elements have been absorbed. The production represents an integration of drama, choreography and song of a kind that was never achieved in the European theatre. The pace has an American briskness and impetuousness. The songs have an American lilt, and the orchestrations, despite the strings, have a smartness and drive and pulse derived from jazz.

As with jazz, it is not so much what it is as the way it is done. Theoretically, any English or European theatre could put on an American musical. In fact, very few of them can, and none with completely satisfactory results. Those that have tried have found it expedient to include American singers in key spots to set the pace and the tone. It was inevitable, for instance, that when, shortly after the London opening of *West Side Story*, word went round that the American cast would stay for only a short time, the advanced ticket sales fell off. They recovered when the rumour was denied.

The heart of the American musical has always been, however, the American song. Not all American song writers have written for the theatre, nor has the theatre or the motion-picture musical always been the medium for their best songs. But the most famous of them—Irving Berlin, Jerome Kern, George Gershwin, Cole Porter, Richard Rodgers, Vincent Youmans, Harold Arlen, Jule Styne, Frank Loesser, Frederick Loewe and Harold Rome—have all been associated primarily with the theatre. Among them they have turned out thousands of good songs—several hundreds of such quality that they have endured for decades, surviving every kind of singer and instrumental combination and yielding countless inspired improvisations by the finest jazz musicians. In this connection one may argue whether or not the typical American song is jazz. But even accepting the proposition that jazz is a way of playing rather than a new music, it remains a fact that the American song, deriving its character from the movement of American life and the cadences of American speech, lends itself to jazz playing as no other music does.

If, in the past decade, song has given way to the production as a whole as the dominant element of the musical, there has been artistic and even musical gain as well as melodic loss. Thirty years ago the typical revue or musical comedy was a loosely constructed affair, a series of skits and production numbers adapted to the talents of the stars around whom a show was built, and capable of absorbing or making use of disparate musical material. It was quite usual for more than one composer to be involved. Material discarded from other shows was often salvaged for a current emergency, and new material would in turn be discarded, only to find employment in a show of the following season. If one thinks in terms of song alone this was probably the golden age of the American musical theatre. Here flourished Berlin, Kern, Porter, Youmans, Schwartz, Rodgers and Gershwin in their young prime, and the result was a bumper crop of memorable songs not equalled in the European theatre since Italian composers, beginning with the later Verdi, were seduced by German example into letting the orchestra dominate the singer. Indeed, this American golden age recalls rather the older Italian opera of the seventeenth and eighteenth centuries when Caldara, Alessandro Scarlatti, Paisiello, Legrenzi, Martini, Piccini, Buononcini, Handel, Gluck and many others produced a treasury of memorable tunes for stereotyped operas about gods and goddesses doubtlessly hardly more memorable otherwise than *Jack o' Lantern* or *Whoopee*, and who shifted material from show to show much as the Americans did two hundred years later. More recently it has come to be expected of a musical that it have a good story and an integrated, homogeneous production, including the music. Gone are the chorus line, the parades of show girls, the comic skits and the hit-or-miss succession of songs and speciality numbers. First Balanchine and then Agnes de Mille, Jerome Robbins and Michael Kidd have shown how to blend choreography and drama. And Rodgers, Porter, Loesser, Loewe, Rome and Leonard Bernstein, among others, have shown how to write a score that is all of a piece with the story and the production. Thus, a song or a production number may now be so much an integral part of a larger whole that it can never have the self-sufficiency of, say, an "Embraceable You".

This move towards integration and sophistication has been so marked that some observers have speculated on when New York will achieve opera. One is tempted to ask: Why should it? What is opera, after all? Is it not merely the name given to the musical theatre in Europe in the seventeenth, eighteenth and nineteenth centuries? In Italy, at least, and to a considerable extent in Germany, it functioned much as the American musical functions today, and much the same rewards were expected of it. No mercy was shown its composers, including even a Verdi, just because what they wrote was called opera and was prompted by high intentions. When their public was displeased with what it got for its money the offending member was hustled off the boards just as ignominiously as last week's Broadway flop.

Technically, all that distinguishes opera from the musical is that opera is music from start to finish, i.e. it has no spoken dialogue; whereas the musical is a play more or less dominated by musical numbers, including ballet. It is a superficial and even inaccurate distinction. Many operas have had spoken dialogue, among them such revered staples of the repertoire as *Die Entführung aus dem Serail*, *The Magic Flute*, *Fidelio* and *Carmen*. Many others have had a kind of dry recitative which is close to the same thing. One is tempted to observe that many a latter-day parlando or recitative opera is considerably less musical than the run-of-the-mill product of Broadway. Nor is the difference a question of subject matter, either. While one instinctively thinks of opera as a serious affair, many operas are lighter and less substantial than *Showboat*, *Oklahoma*, *Lady in the Dark*, or *South Pacific*, not to mention *West Side Story*. One need only cite *The Barber of Seville*, *L'Elisir d'Amore*, *La Serva Padrona*, *Don Pasquale*, *The Secret of Suzanne* and *Gianni Schicchi*. The list could be easily extended.

Music critics are aware of this, of course, and are ready with an answer. They say that the musical does not go as deeply into characterization as opera is expected to do. Howard Taubman, then music critic of the *New York Times*, for instance, found fault with Leonard Bernstein on this count, suggesting that the "Gee, Officer Krupke" episode in *West Side Story* would have been improved by some bitter orchestral commentary. "There is no reason to believe", he wrote, "that he could not have imparted a sting to the scene. But the result might have been music not immediately accessible. The fine line (between Broadway and opera) was neglected; Broadway won out."

One may well ask what is so wrong about immediately accessible music, but Mr. Taubman's less obvious confusion is more fascinating and more pertinent. At the heart of the matter is his concern for an orchestral commentary. It is the clue to his failure, and that of the serious musical community in general, to appreciate the accomplishment of the Broadway composer.

During the so-called romantic period of European music, the public taste for dramatic effects of overwhelming grandeur and intensity, the predilection of both composers and listeners for the transcendental and the overpowering, compelled composers to look to the orchestra for dramatic effects beyond the resources of the mere voice. This went hand in hand with the nineteenth-century trend towards the graphic, the representational and the reflective in music, with the orchestra, or a keyboard substitute, rather than the voice as the preferred instrument, and with harmony and orchestration the preferred media rather than mere melody.

It is not that the orchestral approach and the techniques developed from it did not produce fine operas. They did. But they also took opera a long way from the concepts that had guided Italian opera composers prior to Verdi and such illustrious non-Italians as Handel, Gluck and even Mozart —eloquent as the latter's orchestra often was. The earlier composers thought of song as the natural musical instrument of characterization, as the American composer for the theatre does today. The orchestra was assigned a complementary, supporting or largely decorative role, as is usually the case in the American musical theatre. Later European composers, impelled by the stupendous example of Wagner, and at once more adept with the orchestra than with the voice, and more inventive with harmony than with melody, thought of characterization more and more in terms of the orchestra, the singer articulating the text and providing the visual key.

Today's serious-music critic is inclined to think of the later approach as modern and to the earlier as old-fashioned. This is not to suggest that he also considers the musical as old-fashioned. Indeed, his failure to note the resemblance is his undoing. He may even consider the musical to be modern, and admire it as an example of American folk-art or high-quality entertainment. He forgets that prior to Wagner entertainment was the objective of most opera writing, and he therefore dismisses the musical because it is not derived from the approach to the musical theatre that produced *Tristan und Isolde* and *Otello*.

The resemblance of the musical to older forms of European opera is paralleled by the resemblance of jazz to instrumental music of the eighteenth century, at least in its objectives and methods, if hardly in its sound. Generally speaking, or, at least, musically speaking, and discounting what is called modern music, our century is closer to the eighteenth than to the nineteenth. The style of the American musical, or of the jazz band or combo, is unmistakably American, to be sure, and so is the idiom, but the objective, born of a particular approach to music, is one that an eighteenth-century listener would have understood without difficulty. The contemporary serious composer, impelled by the momentum of the nineteenth century, failed to stay with the pendulum when it started its return journey. The result is that it is not the musical but *The Consul, Vanessa, Peter Grimes, The Rape of Lucretia* and *Troilus and Cressida* that sound old-fashioned, copying, as they do, nineteenth-century European styles and proceeding from a point of view already dated.

Again, it is the question of American *versus* European. The serious-music critic accepts as respectable only that which can be considered a continuation of the European tradition. As far as the theatre is concerned, this means something that he can accept as opera. That which cannot be called opera cannot be taken seriously. The critic and the serious musical community as a whole are taken in by terminology. They are bamboozled in the theatre by the word "opera" just as they are bamboozled in the concert hall by such terms as "symphony", "sonata", "cantata" and "oratorio".

They refuse to acknowledge that what counts is not the form or the label, but the substance; that opera is only a form of musical theatre, that an aria is, after all, only a song and that in our time the United States, which has produced no good operas and probably never will, has for some forty years been experiencing a great era of music in the theatre.

II

It is no longer possible, however, to limit a study of music in the theatre to what has come to be known as "the living theatre". There are also the cinema and television. Compared with the latter the living theatre comprises a small and select area of our theatrical life. It cannot compete successfully with the motion picture, which can present first-class professionals in first-rate material several times a day in scores of cities, towns and villages at once; not to speak of television, which can bring the theatre into the living-room, and which is already superseding the motion picture as the representative theatrical medium of our time. Not only do films and television employ music; they employ more of it than the living theatre ever did—discounting the various forms of specifically musical theatre from opera to musical— and are far more dependent upon it. Indeed, the moving picture and television, in so far as the latter concerns itself with drama, represent, usually and almost inevitably, a new form of musical theatre. Since the television drama broadcast is essentially a motion picture, I shall hereafter refer only to the motion picture, it being understood that what applies to the employment of music in the motion picture also applies or may apply to television.

If the music of the cinema has received even less attention from serious-music critics than the music of the Broadway musical, it can be argued in defence of the critics that in this case, until quite recently at least, it has not merited much. The motion-picture sound-track has been the last functional refuge for the composer of serious music. This excludes, of course, the motion-picture version of the Broadway musical and even the original motion-picture musical, which differ in no musically important respect from the Broadway model. What we are discussing is the musical background for the non-musical film.

This has been the only medium, with the possible exception of ballet, where the descriptive, dramatic and reflective capacities of the later forms of European music could still be turned to profitable use without the need for originality. The imitative flavour of most sound-track music has been no disadvantage, since the music has made no claim to independent existence or distinction; indeed, it has seemed desirable for the music to be associated with previous musical experience, for the spectator normally gives it little attention, and the processes by which he responds to it are almost wholly unconscious. Thus it is that most sound-track music has reminded us of Wagner, Strauss, Debussy, Ravel, the early Stravinsky and Prokofiev, while most modern music that is neither radically neo-classical nor violently dodecaphonic, suggests the sound-track. What is of interest to our discussion, however, is not for the moment the quality of the music—usually a good re-write job, expertly scored and well played—but rather how it got into the theatre in this form, why it has stayed on, and what implications it may have for the future of the musical theatre.

All forms of theatre, from opera through light opera, operetta and musical to spoken drama, have hitherto represented less than completely satisfactory adjustments between the contending interests of the lyrical and the prosaic, or intellectual. The age-old impulse to elevate the dramatic situation from the prosaic to the lyrical by the introduction of music has been inhibited in the so-called legitimate theatre by the impossibility of using music without obscuring the text. An accompanying orchestra gets in the way. The interlude or incidental music founders on the problem of what to do on the stage while the music is going on. Both devices have been employed, to be sure, but the difficulties they create have kept their employment from becoming general. Hence poetry as the next best form of lyrical expression.

The various forms of musical theatre, from opera to musical, represent a solution weighted in favour of music. Here the problems confronting the legitimate theatre are solved automatically. The accompanying orchestra is surmounted by the singing voice. The non-vocal musical interlude finds accommodation on the stage in the form of ballet or a more choreographic style of acting than is acceptable in the legitimate theatre. But a new problem manifests itself: how to accommodate the text?

Originally the narration of the drama was accomplished by dry or accompanied recitative. Full rein was given to the lyrical element at appropriate moments in the form of solo arias and various types of concerted number. In the later stages of operatic evolution the tendency has been to merge the prosaic and the lyrical in a kind of continuous parlando or declamation, delegating ever more lyrical responsibility to the orchestra. This is a compromise designed to give the listener the best of both worlds. In fact, it gives him a little of each, but denies him the best of either.

In the motion picture the problem of reconciling the lyrical and prosaic does not exist, or is easily solved. Electronic devices make it possible to combine music with the speaking voice of the sound-track. The voice can be amplified, the music reduced, or vice-versa, at will. Music can be introduced and withdrawn so inconspicuously that the listener is hardly aware of its arrival, its departure or its effect. Intervals in the action and the text can be filled with music in a way that will contribute to the continuity of each. Music can be used descriptively, dramatically and atmospherically. It can heighten tension, increase suspense and broaden humour. It can elaborate mood. It can be used for all these things, and it is being so used in every picture made nowadays anywhere in the world.

It is pertinent to recall how all this began. Presumably it began with the need to fill the silence of the silent picture and the natural impulse to use music for descriptive and expressive purpose. Many of us can still remember the Saturday night picture in the local hall, with the pianist seated in a corner by the screen playing whatever came into his head or seemed appropriate to what was taking place in the film. The legitimate association of music and picture was recognized by producers and led to the issue of cue sheets to give the pianist or organist a better thought-out, less haphazard guide to what was appropriate than the spur-of-the-moment impulses of his own judgment, ingenious as these often were. In the larger urban houses orchestras and organs played a reasonably well-organized musical score. Then came synchronization and the fully integrated sound-

track, followed shortly by the talking picture. With Al
Jolson's *The Jazz Singer* the way was opened for the highly
organized musical theatre that we have in the motion
picture today.

It may seem odd, in view of the importance of the musical
element, that the motion pictures have produced so little
noteworthy music. One reason, of course, is that its role,
however important, has been, essentially, a secondary one,
and has been so understood by producers, public and
critics. The men who compose for the sound-track have
been content, as we have seen, to exploit the descriptive and
emotionally suggestive devices of European music without
trying to improve upon the European masters, and have
been encouraged to do no more by their employers. By
sticking to familiar styles and devices they have reached the
listener without startling him or diverting his attention from
the picture. The specifically musical film has been rather
better. Its music is, at least, contemporary American. But it
is usually somewhat disappointing as a form. The motion
picture producers and directors have learned to adapt music
to the theatre, but they have not yet learned to adapt the
theatre to music within a strictly motion-picture frame of
reference. The average motion-picture musical is still too
conscious of the stage original, and too faithful to it.

Curiously enough, the exciting hints of what may lie
ahead in this new kind of musical theatre have come, not
from the motion-picture musical, but from straight films.
I am thinking of Elmer Bernstein's scores for *The Man with
the Golden Arm* (big band jazz built around Shorty Rogers'
Giants) and *The Sweet Smell of Success* (chamber jazz built
around Chico Hamilton's Quintet); of Johnny Mandel's
score for *I Want to Live* (featuring Gerry Mulligan); of

John Lewis' scores for *No Sun in Venice* and *Odds Against Tomorrow* (built around the composer's Modern Jazz Quartet), and of Henry Mancini's scores for the *Peter Gunn* television detective series. In each case we have a contemporary story with a score that is of the time, the place and the people. And in each case we have a score that is so much a part of the narrative that score and narrative are quite literally inseparable. Whatever else it may be called, this is musical theatre.

It is important to realize that its music is far closer to what the jazz musician accepts as jazz than is the music of the Broadway musical. This is partly a matter of subject and partly a matter of convention. As a direct descendant of opera and light opera, the musical exhibits a family predilection for exotic subjects, and these do not lend themselves to jazz. Even where the subject is not exotic, as in *Pal Joey*, *Guys and Dolls* and *West Side Story*, and where the setting is modern urban and the language vernacular, the operatic and light-opera heritage is inhibiting. In the motion picture the inhibiting factors are the habits of producers, who content themselves with an inoffensive re-write job, treat music as of only secondary importance and are indifferent to musical quality. These can be turned to advantage. The producer may have no strong musical enthusiasms, but he also has no strong convictions or prejudices. Once persuaded that a score is appropriate and effective, he is not offended that it turns out to be jazz. In turning to jazz the composers are not defiling the treasured memory of any masterpieces, nor defying any tradition save that of inconspicuous mediocrity.

It is, however, a thankless business, and is likely to remain so for many years to come. Even the most enlightened producer gives priority to other elements, and the score must be cut and otherwise tailored to accommodate the narrative and other production considerations. The better composers have recently found a way around this obstacle by recording the whole score and releasing it on LPs. Thus one may hear a lot more of the music John Lewis wrote for *No Sun in Venice* and *Odds Against Tomorrow* on records than is audible in the final form of the film.

Nor can the composers count on critical appreciation. The serious critics take a patronizing view of the songs from the musical, but at least they are aware of the institution and the most famous names associated with it. Of what is going on musically today in motion pictures they are totally and presumably blissfully ignorant. The motion-picture critics, in whose province the pictures fall, rarely notice the score and even more rarely mention it. The Academy Awards go year after year to the established composers of conventional sound-tracks, the Steiners, Newmans, Tiomkins, Roszas, etc. Only the jazz critics are aware of what is afoot, and since they themselves have no status, their praise contributes little to the composer's esteem outside the tight fraternity of jazz intellectuals.

This is unfortunate but probably inevitable. In a sense this new form of musical theatre has sneaked up on us. It has achieved acceptance without being recognized, and as between acceptance and recognition the former is the more important. Recognition can wait. The decisive thing about music in the motion picture is not that it is good, bad or indifferent, but that it is essential. What matters is that the combination of a reel or film and a sound-track has opened the way to a new form of musical theatre, and that the form is already with us. Musical evolution will determine its ultimate use. The scores I have mentioned indicate a trend from the older European to the newer American music, but it is no more than a trend. The associations of the emotional and descriptive devices of European music are still vivid and effective in their inconspicuous supporting function, and their usefulness is by no means at an end.

Moreover, the emphasis to be given the prosaic and lyrical elements respectively, and to the relationship between the two, will always be in question. Some pictures will be more musical than others. But the forms will no longer evolve as compromise solutions of the acoustical problems that have hitherto determined the various forms of the musical theatre. The motion picture can have it both ways. The text may have music, and the music a text. There will be music in the theatre and theatre in music. Just the turn of a knob in the sound engineer's hands, and formerly insuperable problems are no more. All that is needed is for producers and composers and critics to recognize what they have already accepted and set about the business of providing the contemporary form with an appropriately contemporary music. Elmer Bernstein, Johnny Mandel, John Lewis and Henry Mancini have shown the way.

# DIRECTION

IN MY INTRODUCTION to these chapters I suggested that we might examine the evolutionary crises of serious music and jazz, or, to use the terminology which I prefer, of European music and American music, and attempt to arrive at some general conclusions relating each to the other and applicable to the crisis of musical evolution as a whole.

I also suggested, paradoxically, it seemed, that, while things are probably worse than most people think, they are by no means as bad as they appear. I meant, of course, that, while serious music has produced little of any importance since the end of the first two decades of the century, and is unlikely to produce any more, American music has produced and is still producing a new kind of music of such world-wide appeal, and frequently of such quality, that our century may well go down in the history of western music as the most decisive since the seventeenth.

The real paradox is that the very thought of such a thing provokes among the musical élite, not self-congratulation, but hostility, incredulity and, at best, dismay. It is not that the serious composer, the serious critic and the serious-music audience are not progressive. Indeed, they have carried progressiveness to dogmatic and sometimes—as with electronic music and the twelve-tone aberrations of Boulez and Nono—to ludicrous lengths, and have been open-minded to the point where simple-minded would often seem to be the more appropriate adjective. But it is a progress—if such it can be called—of their own, or at least

of their composers' excogitation, and has been proclaimed
without reference to the cash customers, even of their own
products. It is a kind of defensive progressiveness, designed
to convince the onlooker that fundamentally all is well and
that this generation's sceptics will be the next generation's
Hanslicks. In other words, our serious-music progressives
are, at heart, reactionaries. The mere thought of American
indigenous music as being the truly vital contemporary
music of the century, the mere thought of jazz, of the songs
of the American musical, of the motion-picture sound-track
—of popularly rooted music, if you will—as being, not only
music worth taking seriously, but even as the new bearers
of the main stream of western music, is a defiance of all the
canons of their musical faith.

To accept such a thought would be to challenge the
barrier of folklore and superstition that protects the contemporary serious composer from the modest requirement
of pleasing his listeners or even of addressing them in a
language they understand. It would be to suggest that
identification with a quality category is no evidence of
quality, and that the writing of serious music is not synonymous with the writing of music worth taking seriously. It
would even be to challenge the critical propriety of our
present major categories, namely, serious and popular. It
would be, finally, to suggest that music whose purpose is to
entertain and to please, may be superior to the music of
composers who regard entertainment and the giving of
pleasure as ignoble objectives and who are, for the most part,
apparently incapable of writing agreeable music.

We may be sure that it will not be accepted, least of all by
serious composers and serious-music critics whose reputations as authorities on music would hardly gain lustre by

the canonization of a music which has been with us for fifty
years, but about which they know little and care less. They
cannot, however, prevent a gradual realization on the part
of the general public, and particularly the record-buying
public, that we are confronted by a new kind of music, a
new idiom and, possibly, a new approach to music that
cannot for ever be dismissed as merely popular and therefore
worthless.

How this realization comes about will depend to a
considerable degree upon what happens in American music
in the next ten to twenty years. This is what I mean when I
speak of a crisis of direction. Jazz has emerged from its age
of innocence, but it has not yet achieved intellectual maturity. It is an astonishing adolescent, but an adolescent,
nevertheless, and it has a tendency to behave accordingly.
I have mentioned its snobbery. For the past few years there
have also been much vain virtuosity, much self-conscious
striving for originality (usually ending only in eccentricity),
a lot of mawkish preoccupation with self-expression, and
a tiresome pose of supercilious disapproval of musicians
who court their public.

Jazz musicians have been encouraged in these attitudes,
partly beatnik, but mostly borrowed from the romance of
European music, by a new fraternity of jazz critics whose
members are aware of and, quite reasonably, resent the
inferior status of the jazz musician. But they also believe,
apparently, that the way to improve it is for him to emulate
the serious composer in his attitude towards the paying
public, and in the production of a pretentiously ugly music
distinguished from the modern serious variety only by the
beat and the instrumentation. This kind of criticism has
been called, most happily, I think, "bearded bigotry",

referring to the tendency of some of its practitioners to wear their long hair on their chins.

In other words, the serious composer's superior status tempts a certain kind of immature jazz musician to ape him and a certain kind of immature jazz critic to applaud the mimicry. Fortunately, his very lack of status should save the jazz musician from the serious composer's fate of being more pampered than loved. The serious composer fails to please his audience, but his status protects him from uninhibited criticism and the hoots of an outraged public. This status was not gained by anything he himself has written. The jazz musician is unlikely to gain it by imitation, and the certain loss of his paying public may be counted upon either to bring him to his senses or eliminate him from the scene.

Not all jazz musicians have succumbed so readily to these pitfalls of adolescence, although the worst offenders have inevitably been accorded the most attention and been made the object of flattery as innovators, pioneers and original geniuses. A majority have kept faith with the general jazz public, and the best of them have shown how jazz can gain from European music without committing itself to the serious composer's presumptuous attitudes and inviting his lamentable predicaments.

While it is obviously risky to predict the musical future, the evolution of jazz from the New Orleans or Chicago jazz band of the early twenties to the big band of today has been so fast that momentum alone might reasonably be expected to carry it further in the same direction. This direction, despite such a spectacular and unpalatable deviation as rock 'n roll, or such a retrogressive phenomenon as the New Orleans revivalist movement of the forties, runs clearly from the primitive to the sophisticated, from the simple to the complex, from the uninhibited and spontaneous to the consciously refined and artfully calculated. At one pole we have the modest basic ensemble of cornet, trombone, clarinet, piano, tuba, banjo and drums, or a variation of it, with its heavy two-beat rhythm and its collective improvisation within a pattern of rudimentary diatonic harmonies. At the other we have an imposing ensemble of sixteen pieces or more, with saxophone and brass choirs sustained and propelled by a rhythm group of piano, double-bass, guitar and drums, and a repertoire of arrangements and original compositions, often exquisitely refined in terms of both harmony and instrumentation, and requiring a very high standard of virtuosity, musicianship and rehearsal. Or we find the small combo—trio, quartet, quintet, etc.—playing music of similar or even greater complexity, but sacrificing the variety and range of colour and dynamics that only the big band can provide. It is the jazz equivalent of chamber music, and appeals similarly to the more discriminating among the jazz public.

The impulses that have propelled jazz across the great distance separating these two poles did not all come from the rhythm section. Many of them came from European music, to which jazz musicians were exposed when their music emerged from the comparative isolation of the New Orleans slums. Many more came from both white and Negro musicians, sufficiently educated musically to have absorbed the conventions and some of the arts of European music, who were attracted to jazz and joined the ranks of its practitioners, bringing with them their greater knowledge, particularly of harmony and instrumentation. From the ensuing fermentation emerged the hybrid white bands of the twenties, such as those of Whiteman, Lopez, Lewis and Goldkette, and the first great Negro bands of Moten, Lunceford, Henderson and Ellington. There followed the "swing era", dominated by the bands of Goodman, the Dorsey brothers, Glenn Miller, Woody Herman and Count Basie, and ultimately the superbly organized big bands of today, of which Basie's is generally conceded to be the finest example.

On the evidence of the past decade it appears unlikely, however, that the future of jazz lies primarily with further development of the big band, at least as a fixed institution. Larger ensembles will always tempt the jazz arranger and composer, but they will probably be brought together for special purposes and short periods. As a permanent organization big bands are too expensive and, for those who play in them, too anonymous. Both the individual musician's desire to achieve fame and a unique identity, and the jazz audience's enthusiasm for individual accomplishment, favour the small combo. This happy coincidence of professional aspiration and public preference, plus economic considerations, suggest that the small combo will carry the mainstream of jazz for some time to come.

This, plus the fact that the jazz audience today increasingly likes listening better than dancing, may well prove to be the turning point in the jazz musician's quest of status. The big band is difficult for the serious-music lover to accept. No matter how fine the arrangements, how stunning the virtuosity of the players, how fine the ensemble achievement, it strikes him as too noisy and too obstreperous. It is even more difficult for him to accept if it plays for dancing, which the serious-music lover regards as a degrading employment. The small combo, on the other hand, with its comparative sobriety, its lower decibel count, its harmonic and contrapuntal sophistication, its refined virtuosity and its intent listeners, is at once less frightening and less foreign. There are probably many serious-music lovers, particularly among the younger generation, who can relate John Lewis, surrounded by his colleagues of the Modern Jazz Quartet, to Haydn, surrounded by colleagues from Prince Esterhazy's orchestra in the performance of trios and quartets; but who could never stomach a comparison of Count Basie's band with the orchestra at Coethen for which Bach wrote the Brandenburg Concertos.

That the increasing sophistication of the instrumental jazz groups and the increasing refinement of the jazz virtuoso have been accompanied by or contributed to an increasing sophistication and refinement in composition would seem to go without saying. They have been achieved, of course, at the expense of spontaneous improvisation, one of early jazz's most engaging distinctions. Here the evolutionary trends of European and American music are obviously running parallel. Improvisation was lost to European music when the conventions of composition and the requirements of instrumental organization became too complex to accommodate it, and it is slowly disappearing from jazz for the same reasons.

There has also been a parallel history of abuse. Artful variation, elaboration and ornamentation of a familiar theme are one thing, and the best jazz musicians have accomplished them with marvellous invention and exemplary artistry, but licentious distortion is something else. The problems of instrumental organization may have put an end to improvisation in European instrumental music, but in the opera house the end came when singers mangled

the composer's materials beyond recognition. Improvisation
has not ended in jazz yet, but the be-bop era, when musicians
playing a standard melody first discarded the melody to
improvise freely over the chords, and then went on to alter
the chords, made it plain that a line had to be drawn. The
alternative was composition, and the trend since then has
been in that direction, with the repertoire breaking down
into the now familiar categories of "standards" and
"originals".

Jazz composition, as opposed to arrangements of "standards", would seem to provide the possibility of escape from
a variety of conventions which have hitherto retarded the
progress of jazz from the primitive to the sophisticated. In
the matter of form, for instance, it offers a release from the
"theme and variations" (or, in jazz terminology, sequence
of "choruses") which has been dominant in jazz since the
beginning, and which, in recent years, with each musician
demanding his turn as soloist, has often resulted in succes-
sions of solos with routine "comping" accompaniment and
a corresponding neglect of the ensemble. This sort of thing
in the hands of any but the very finest soloists, can be dull,
particularly when the soloists are double bass players,
flutists and drummers. One may hope that the growing
influence of composers may persuade trumpeters to fall back
below high C, saxophonists to cease honking, double-bass
players to prefer anonymity and drummers to live with the
notion that their instruments are not melodic.

The prospects for the jazz composer compared with those
for the contemporary serious composer are not bad. For
one thing, he is not faced with the same harmonic inhibi-
tions. Without any help from theoreticians, jazz has worked
out an accommodation with harmony as it existed in Euro-

pean music at the turn of the century. This accommodation
can most simply be defined as the acceptance of the seventh
rather than the triad as the basic chord. It implies, of course,
a concept of key relationships radically different from that
which governed composition in European music in the
eighteenth and nineteenth centuries, but the older concepts
had lost most of their validity as a result of the harmonic
advances of Wagner and Strauss, and the jazz procedure
seems to represent no more than an instinctive rationalization of an accomplished harmonic fact. Curiously, in
achieving this rationalization, jazz musicians have worked
out a system of chord symbols which, in its purpose if not
in the precise meanings of the symbols, resembles the figured
bass of older European music.

What saves the jazz composer from the harmonic predicament of the serious composer is that he is not required
to be harmonically original. Given a music of different
character and purpose, he can use an inherited harmony in
an original way, exploiting such unique resources as the
jazz drummer, the jazz double-bassist and the ability of the
jazz instrumental-virtuoso to excel within the framework
of pulsative composition. Neither the jazz drummer nor the
jazz double-bassist has a counterpart in the symphony
orchestra, or any other European-type ensemble. The
instruments themselves are there, of course, but they are so
differently played that comparison is impossible. What has
been done with these two instruments—if one can speak of
the jazz drummer's apparatus as a single instrument—is a
measure of the distance jazz has covered in forty years,
both from its own humble beginnings and from the conventions of European music. One has only to compare the
tuba of early New Orleans jazz with the double-bass as

played today by a Ray Brown or a Percy Heath; the banjo with the guitar as played by Freddie Green or Tal Farlow; the drums as played by Baby Dodds with the drums as played today by Max Roach, Jo Jones or Ed Thigpen, to sense the magnitude of the accomplishment. What the jazz composer has additionally at his disposal in the form of saxophones, trumpets and trombones, or rather in the form of a style of playing them evolved by scores of inventive virtuosos over the years, would seem to be too obvious to warrant emphasis.

If jazz continues in this direction we may anticipate a gradual narrowing of the gap which has for so long separated it from serious music. By this I do not mean to suggest that serious music will begin to absorb jazz. It is the other way round. The inner pulsation of jazz is foreign to the character and objectives of serious music. There is nothing about the melodic forms and harmonic structures of serious music, however, that is irreconcilable with the character and objectives of jazz. The jazz composer can draw upon the techniques of serious music at will. His problem is not what he can use, but how he may use it. His most frequent error in the past has been to become too "symphonic". Artie Shaw, Stan Kenton, Bill Russo, Sauter-Finegan and even Duke Ellington have fallen into it from time to time, but the inevitable loss of the jazz audience, with no compensating gain among any other, acts as a safeguard.

Thus, paradoxical though it may seem, we may anticipate fewer ventures into symphonic jazz as the gap between jazz and serious music is reduced. Symphonic jazz was a tempting prospect as long as the difference between jazz and European music was thought of in terms of serious and popular. Once it is generally acknowledged that the differ-

ence is generic, that a gap there will always be, however
much it may be narrowed, then it must also be recognized
that symphonic jazz is a contradiction in terms. Moreover,
as jazz gains in status, its composers will be less tempted to
try symphonic writing as a bid for respectability. We may
also hope that they will be less susceptible to the empty
fashions of serious music's *avant-garde* reactionaries. There
is no brighter future for the jazz musician in atonality and
dodecaphony than there is for the serious composer. He
may derive a semblance of vitality from the beat, but the
beat alone is not enough.

What counts in any music is song. The jazz musician
need only remember what the serious composer has long
forgotten, namely, that the purpose of the musician is to
sing, that the discipline within which he must work is his
listeners' concept of song, and that his ultimate fulfilment is
not just self-expression, which any fool can manage after a
fashion, but rather the initiation of his listeners into an
experience of the beautiful. This requires a knowledge and
acceptance of the listener's language. The objective of the
musician's song is communication, and it cannot be accomplished without giving the listener an even break.

# BIBLIOGRAPHY

1. Oswald Spengler, *The Decline of the West*, Allen & Unwin (London) 1922, Alfred A. Knopf (New York) 1946.
2. Artur Honegger, *Je suis Compositeur*, Editions du Conquistador (Paris) 1951.
3. Roger Sessions, *The Musical Experience*, Oxford (London) 1951.
4. Aaron Copland, *Music and Imagination*, Oxford (London) 1953.
5. Arnold Schönberg, *Style and Idea*, Williams & Norgate (London) 1951.
6. Karl Geiringer, *Haydn a Creative Life in Music*, Allen & Unwin (London) 1947.
7. Emily Anderson, *Letters of Mozart and His Family*, Macmillan (London) 1938.
8. *International Cyclopedia of Music and Musicians*, Dodd, Mead & Co. (New York) 1939.
9. Ernst Krenek, *Studies in Counterpoint based on the 12-Tone Technique*, G. Schirmer (New York) 1940.
10. Paul Hindemith, *A Composer's World*, Oxford (London) 1952.
11. Igor Stravinsky, *Poetics of Music*, Oxford (London) 1947.
12. Ernst Krenek, *Selbstdarstellung*, Atlantis-Verlag (Zürich) 1948.
13. Theodore Stravinsky, *The Message of Igor Strawinsky*, Boosey & Hawkes (London) 1953.
14. Eduard Hanslick, *Vienna's Golden Years of Music: 1850-1900*, edited and translated by Henry Pleasants, Gollancz (London) 1951.
15. Grove's *Dictionary of Music and Musicians*, Macmillan (London) 1954.
16. Henry F. Chorley, *Thirty Years' Musical Recollections*, edited by Ernest Newman, Alfred A. Knopf (New York) 1927.
17. Hector Berlioz, *Memoirs*, edited by Ernest Newman, Heffer (Cambridge) 1948.
18. Ernest Newman, *Fact and Fiction about Wagner*, Cassell (London) 1931.
19. André Hodeir, *Jazz: Its Evolution and Essence*, Secker & Warburg (London) 1956.
20. Vernon Duke, *Passport to Paris*, Little Brown & Co. (Boston and Toronto) 1955.
21. Paul Henry Lang, *Music in Western Civilization*, J. M. Dent (London) 1942.
22. Adam Carse, *The Orchestra in the Eighteenth Century*, Heffer (Cambridge) 1950.